When Santa
Was a Shaman

The Shadow of the Shaman

"All those who celebrate life and humanity, who resist the inroads of fundamentalist religious thinking and generally 'question authority,' will delight in Tony van Renterghem's detailed and diverting research into the Olde Religion, Pan, solstice ceremonies, and the Tree of Fire. His reclamation of Santa Claus as a direct shamanic descendant will make a great gift to put in the stocking of a special someone."

— Janette Rainwater, Ph.D.
Author of *You're in Charge:
A Guide to Becoming Your Own Therapist*

The beloved image of the American Santa Claus represents only the tip of an ancient iceberg. The origins of Santa Claus and the Christmas tree stretch back many thousands of years, to when the mythic figure known as Santa Claus was a tribal shaman and keeper of fire. The Christmas tree itself is the last vestige of the myth of the Tree of Fire, whose burning branches first brought the gift of fire to our ancestors.

Why have these myths resurfaced again and again all over the world, despite the passage of time and repression by many hostile cultures and religions? By which mysterious paths did they travel to arrive in the twentieth century? And why are they still important today?

Tony van Renterghem has done ten years of research into these questions and more. Explore his fascinating findings, which trace the evolution of these myths from prehistoric times to the present. And rediscover the myths of our old Pagan past, which refuse to die—even in the midst of our commercialized culture!

"... a source of profound insight into the process of mythic transformation of pagan belief and practice, yielding across time the lovable image of robust benevolence so delightful to children of all ages."

— Rabbi Dr. Benjamin Herson
Founder, The Raoul Wallenberg Institute of Ethics

About the Author

Tony van Renterghem was born in Amsterdam in the Netherlands in 1919. He has studied history, art, photography, motion-picture arts, and contract law. He speaks Dutch, English, French, and German. Trained as one of the last mounted cavalry officers, he served eight years in the Netherlands Armed Forces, including four years in the resistance during the German World War II occupation, for which he was condemned to death, but escaped. At the end of the war he served on Prince Bernhard's General Staff of the Netherlands Army. He later organized local and foreign exhibits for the Dutch government and was active in international politics.

In 1948, he emigrated to the United States where he spent thirty years in the motion picture and television industry, serving as assistant cameraman, actor, assistant, advisor, and writer for several major studios. As Hollywood's top historical researcher, he was technical advisor and the personal assistant to director George Stevens, Sr. on such pictures as *The Diary of Anne Frank* and the biblical epic *The Greatest Story Ever Told*.

Now semi-retired, he continues to work as a writer and consultant. He lives in the Netherlands with his wife.

To Write to the Author

If you wish to contact the author or would like more information about this book, please write to the author in care of Llewellyn Worldwide, and we will forward your request. Both the author and the publisher appreciate hearing from you and learning of your enjoyment of this book and how it has helped you. Llewellyn Worldwide cannot guarantee that every letter written to the author can be answered, but all will be forwarded. Please write to:

Tony van Renterghem
℅ Llewellyn Worldwide
P.O. Box 64383-K765, St. Paul, MN 55164-0383, U.S.A.

Please enclose a self-addressed, stamped envelope or $1.00 to cover costs.
If outside the U.S.A., enclose international postal reply coupon.

When Santa Was a Shaman

The Ancient Origins of Santa Claus &
The Christmas Tree

Tony van Renterghem

1995
Llewellyn Publications
St. Paul, MN 55164-0383 U.S.A.

FIRST EDITION
First Printing, 1995

Cover design: Anne Marie Garrison
Color insert design: Anne Marie Garrison
Book design, layout, and editing: Jessica Thoreson

Illustration credits begin on page 183

Publisher's note: Much in this book is based on the author's personal research and comparisons with still-existing primitive cultures. Necessarily, the author has extended the work with conjecture in areas where field research is still limited. Future studies may disprove or confirm some of the author's theories. The ideas and opinions presented herein are not necessarily those of the publisher, who encourages originality and diversity in esoteric study and practice.

Library of Congress Cataloging-in-Publication Data
Renterghem, Tony van, 1919-
    When Santa was a shaman: the ancient origins of Santa
    Claus & the Christmas tree / Tony van Renterghem. -- 1st ed.
      p.   cm.
    Includes bibliographical references and index.
    ISBN 1-56718-765-X (trade pbk.: alk. paper)
    1. Santa Claus -- History. 2. Christmas trees -- History.
    3. Shamanism -- Europe, Northern. 4. Europe, Northern --
    Religion.
    I. Title.
GT4992.R56   1995
394.2'663--dc20   95-20306
                                            CIP

Printed in the United States of America

Llewellyn Publications
A Division of Llewellyn Worldwide, Ltd.
P.O. Box 64383, St. Paul, MN 55164-0383

Contents

Part I

fascination with death, sin, and afterlife. Nature spirit versus gods in man's image. The deification of mythical heroes and chiefs. The Celtic, Nordic, Roman, and Christian authority versus the enduring pagan traditions.

Time, a relatively modern concept. From solar time to Roman calendars. The card game; an early calendar. How the same harvest/slaughter feast ended up months apart in different areas. How differences in climate affected changes in the dates of celebrations. The 1582 calendar changes. Why the Pilgrims hated Xmas. When the day started at sunset rather than at midnight.

The incredibly old memory of the gift of fire. The fear of losing the sun. The sacrifice of the burning tree; the first deal with god. Evergreens, harbingers of the rebirth of life. Mistletoe, symbol of lightning, fire, and sex. "The Tree of Fire" as a worldwide celebration. The Christian Church's battle against tree worship, fire sacrifices, and procreation feasts.

Part II

Searching for the origins of Santa Claus, starting off with a 10,000-year-old shaman—poet, procreational master of ceremonies, scientist, philosopher, and healer. The sexual aspects of the shaman and the post-pagan world. The besom (broom) as a symbol of pagan procreation.

Acknowledgements

I would hereby like to thank the following for their assistance in researching aspects of this story:

Dr. R. M. Staal of the Katerijnen Convent Museum at Utrecht, the Netherlands.

Dr. van der Meer, historian of the Amsterdam Rijksmuseum, the Netherlands.

Mr. T. Ruitens of the Dutch National School Museum at Rotterdam, the Netherlands.

Dr. Gerard Rooyakkers of the Amsterdam P. J. Meertens-Institute of Folklore, Dialectology, and Names Department of the Royal Netherlands Academy of Science.

Mr. Appel of the town of Denekamp's Department of Folklore, the Netherlands.

Mr. Theo Timmer of the Open Boek store on the Dutch island of Texel, for filling me in on ancient island customs.

I'd also like to thank the many other individuals who, over the years and in many countries, gave me little bits of anthropological and folkloric information to help me solve this puzzle of the origins of Santa Claus and the Xmas tree, and those who expressed such interest and encouragement in my work-in-progress.

And, above all, my wife, Susanne, for her help and support along the way.

Yes, Virginia, There is a Santa Claus

In 1897, Virginia O'Hanlon wrote to the New York Sun:

Dear Editor: I am eight years old. Some of my friends say there is no Santa Claus. Papa says, "If you see it in THE SUN it's so." Please tell me the truth, is there a Santa Claus?

This is part of the reply that appeared in the paper:

Virginia, your friends are wrong. They have been affected by the skepticism of a skeptical age. They think that nothing can be which is not comprehensible by their little minds. All minds, Virginia, whether they be men's or children's, are little. In this great universe of ours man is a mere insect, an ant, in his intellect as compared with the boundless world about him, as measured by the intelligence capable of grasping the whole of truth or knowledge.

Yes, Virginia, there is a Santa Claus. He exists as certainly as love and generosity and devotion exist, and you know that they abound and give to your life its highest beauty and joy. Alas! how dreary would the world be if there were no Santa Claus! It would be as dreary as if there were no Virginias. There would be no childlike faith then, no poetry, no romance to make tolerable this existence. We should have no enjoyment, except in sense and sight.

Not believe in Santa Claus? Nobody sees Santa Claus, but that is no sign that there is no Santa Claus. The most real things in the world are those that neither children nor men can see. Nobody can conceive or imagine all the wonders there are, unseen and unseeable in the world.

You can tear apart a baby's rattle and see what makes the noise inside, but there is a veil covering the unseen world which not the strongest man, nor even the united strength of all the strongest men that ever lived, could tear apart. Only faith, poetry, love, romance, can push aside that curtain and view and picture the supernatural beauty and glory beyond. Is it all real? Ah, Virginia, in all this world there is nothing else real and abiding.

No Santa Claus! Thank God he lives and lives forever. A thousand years from now, Virginia, nay, ten thousand years from now, he will continue to make glad the heart of childhood.

—Francis P. Church, *The New York Sun,* 1897

Introduction

If you wander the streets of London, Paris, New York, or even Tokyo during the month of December, you will see a multitude of Xmas[1] trees and jolly Santa Clauses, boosting the sales of a multitude of consumer goods, many of which, by the way, this world would be far better off without. Why do we do this; what is this myth? Where do rituals such as those of the Xmas tree with its burning

1. *I use the spelling "Christmas" in referring to the celebration of the mass held in memory of the birth of Christ and related Christian rituals. The word "Xmas" denotes the joyous pagan celebrations.*

candles, and of the figure of Santa Claus spring from? Aren't they a kind of children's story, like Donald Duck or Mickey Mouse, rather than myths? Do they really matter? What's the big deal?

Most of us no longer have the vaguest idea of what a true myth is, let alone from where these particular old customs originated, or what these figures and symbols once stood for. Yet, imprinted on our subconscious minds are vague memories of mythical rituals, vestiges of which we still perform and pass on to our offspring, without realizing why. Most people don't know that the Xmas tree and Santa Claus are incredibly ancient myths and rituals. They are part of Western man's roots; possibly your roots. Okay, you may say, what's so important about roots?

We are living in a state of emotional instability, in a time of unthought-of exponential change and culture shock. Our minds are overloaded by ever-increasing new input, while we somehow try to survive within the wreckage of what once was the traditional family. Swept away in a vast maelstrom of new technology, violence, rapidly-growing different cultures and their new religious fundamentalism, many of us sense a desperate need to retain our own cultural values as a matter of psychological survival in what seems to have become an alien world. Yet if we do not reacquaint ourselves with these "roots" now, what little remains will gradually be erased from our memory and will be forever lost.

Rituals and myths, such as those involving Xmas and Santa Claus, are among the few remaining links to our ancient roots; they are part of the most tenacious and most important myth of all—the story of man's first awareness of being part of something greater than himself and of the shattering memory of the conquest of fire; that fiery instant which totally changed the fate of mankind.

Modern society is slowly and reluctantly reawakening to the fact that we must learn to live in harmony with our environment and with nature, or perish. This concept, in which the earth is known as "Gaia," recognizes our world—and in a larger sense, the entire

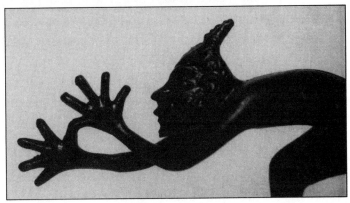

Above: Shamanic prankster/jokester figure, used as an ornament throughout this book. *Below:* Detail of the figure. As the impersonator of nature, the shaman often portrayed its fickleness and unpredictability, making fun of "the best laid plans of mice and men." In certain areas, he is depicted with goat horns. The excessively long tail is a fairly recent genteel replacement of the erect penis as a fertility symbol.

In parts of Belgium during the nineteenth century, there were uprisings by poor laborers against the church and the wealthy land owners. These Robin Hood-like men were called *Bokkerijders* ("goat riders"). They wore horned masks, operated out of the forest, and in their rituals gave the "horned" hand signal (a fist with the little and index fingers up). The church and local gentry made these men out to be worshipers of Satan. They were not; they still believed in Herne's Olde Religion. In Slavic countries, such as the former Yugoslavia, Saint Nicholas' Dark Helper is a smallish figure dressed in black, with horns and large, pointed, red ears. He dances around and scares the children. He is closely related to this tiny, present-day Russian figurine of Herne/Pan as the shamanic prankster, and is, according to the Russian salesperson, "not scary, but friendly, since he is from before Satan."

Universe—as one living entity of which we are only a small, yet vital, part.

The so-called primitive humans were very much in tune with Gaia, and their earliest religious concepts reflected their symbiosis with nature and with the forces of creation, life, and death. Their shaman/medicine-man was the link (the popular modern term would be "channel") between them and Gaia. When he appeared ceremoniously and spoke as shaman, they saw him not only as possessed by the voice and spirit of Gaia, but as Gaia incarnate. Gaia never died, so man never really died, either; reabsorbed by Gaia, people continued to exist. See the shaman, and you see Gaia; eat your bread, and you are eating part of Gaia; drink your wine, and you are drinking part of Gaia. Listen, dance to the beat of the drum and the tune of the pipes, and you hear and feel Gaia. Dance on, make love, and you not only feel Gaia, you let it enter you; both you and Gaia are reborn—you and Gaia are one!

Then came that all-important instant in man's early history: his first knowledge, the discovery of the use of fire. It gave man an advantage over other animals; it was also his first step away from Gaia. Ever since, man has seen in himself a god-like superiority, which allows him to control and master his environment. This event is remembered in the Bible as the original sin, and is also reflected in Western man's arrogant tendency to see and portray his God in the image of a male human of his own race.

Two ancient myths still exist to remind us of that momentous instant in man's past:

1. The myth of the Tree of Fire: man's oldest fire ritual. Our Xmas tree ceremony is one of the last vestiges of that ancient mystery.

2. The persistent, vague memory of the ancient shaman, who helped man to stay in harmony with Gaia. Today, the commercial Santa Claus is his pathetic relic.

Why are these ancient myths and rituals still important? Philosophers have always understood that we are more than ourselves, that we are part of a larger entity and that this larger entity is part of us; that we are not just one life spent in a void, but are part of the past as well as of the present and future. Consider the cells in our bodies, which die off every seven years. Without such cells there would be no body, yet the body as a whole continues to exist in spite of this constant changing of cells. In the same way, our generation is part of the "body" of our entity; an entity composed of our race, culture, nationality, and history. It existed before us, it grows and changes with us, and it will continue to exist after us, as a component of that larger entity, our world, and, in turn, our universe. It is a little like a regularly updated computer diskette which keeps on working in spite of the fact that parts of the computer are constantly being replaced.

What does all this have to do with our present-day lives? Far more than one might think. Let's use the following example: during the winter holidays we may all be sitting around a cozy open fire sharing a warm drink after having laid our presents under the Christmas tree, a tree which we have just decorated and lit with candles. Have you ever wondered why we do this and why we consider this "cozy"? After all, open fireplaces are hardly efficient or cost-effective; nor does bringing in a messy, needle-shedding pine tree, decorated with glittery junk, serve any conceivable practical purpose. And why do some of us dress up as a bearded old man, pretending to be some peculiar fellow named Santa Claus?

What is the purpose of these odd rituals and why do they give us "comfort and joy," as the old Christmas carol tells us? As with so many customs, the purpose has long since been forgotten, yet we continue to perform the ritual and feel good about it, because we were culturally and ritually programmed millennia ago to do so and to enjoy it.

The purpose of rituals can be forgotten in a very short span of time. Take, for instance, the American ritual of Memorial Day; a legal holiday in the United States, originally in remembrance of the war dead of the Civil War, and later extended to honor all war dead. Barely a century has gone by since this ritual was first instituted, yet eighty percent of Americans have forgotten for whom this memorial was originally established, and a good fifty percent only think of it as an occasion for sports, games, or a family picnic. Even so, this event is observed, and, unless some new culture wipes out this existing one, it will probably go on being observed for centuries, long after the citizens have forgotten why this celebration existed in the first place.

The more ancient the ritual or taboo, the longer it seems to continue to exist. What then, exactly, is such a ritual and "taboo"?

Long before the existence of speech, when man's ancestors lived together in small groups or clans, they developed two closely related ways of maintaining and repeating actions beneficial to the survival of the clan (man is not the only species to do so; certain other mammals, such as wolves, do so also). Before speech existed, they developed the ritual, best described as "monkey see, monkey do"—a ceremony in which one copies the actions of others—and the taboo, the forbidden behaviour; the "Thou Shalt Not!" These were not—and are not—taught on a rational basis, but were "programmed"[2] into our subconscious from the moment of birth; the ritual by the repeated example of the clan, and the taboo by the threat of severe punishment or even death.

With the coming of speech also came the new concept of "why?" (the first questioning of authority). This led to the development of the myth: a poetic, often fictional, allegorical story explaining the origin and need for the ritual or taboo. With time, a myth, ritual, or taboo may not remain valid or beneficial to a clan, yet due to the way in which it has been programmed into the culture, it proves to be almost impossible to erase, as long as even traces of the clan remain in existence. Also, a different clan or nation can

2. *Bootcamp training and totalitarian regimes still use similar approaches.*

come under the cultural influence of another and, in so doing, absorb and perpetuate the rituals and taboos of that conquering nation, seemingly without any reason, other than seeing such rituals and taboos as a part of the trappings of the power structure they admire and try to copy.

Carl Jung, and more recently, Joseph Campbell, taught us how myths and rituals connect us to the childhood of mankind, with subconscious ancient memories of clan gatherings and the warm safety of flaming campfires. They also taught us how these myths and rituals give us necessary rites of passage and points of reference which help us navigate our way through life, supplying our clans with a sense of continuity from long before our own birth, and far into a future where we, as individuals, will be long gone.

Today, the Christmas Nativity symbolizes the Christian Church's worship of the birth of Jesus of Nazareth, in whom they see the Christ ("the Anointed One"), the Son of God, whereas Santa Claus, the Tree of Fire, and the pagan Winter Solstice celebration are far older remnants of an ancient pagan, mythological, and cultural past; its roots are so ancient and buried so deeply that its origins have almost been forgotten. Yet, oddly, this pagan Xmas feast, even more strongly than Nativity pageants, has come to embody the joyous faith many of us have in the principles of love, generosity, and caring taught us by Jesus, the young Jewish rabbi (teacher) and carpenter from Nazareth, who called himself the Son of Man. No celebration comes closer to the spirit of Jesus' social teachings than Xmas.

Since the myth of the Nativity is so well-known, this book will deal exclusively with the rediscovery of the tenacious myths of our much earlier, pagan, cultural past. Simply consider this a kind of ancestral detective story, a search for roots, to be read near a cozy fire on a cold winter night.

Much in this book is, by necessity, based on conjecture and on comparisons with still-existing primitive cultures. I, consequently, expect that future studies may disprove or confirm some of my findings. I hope, however, that this effort will encourage others to research this subject in greater depth.

—TONY VAN RENTERGHEM, 1995

Note: Throughout this book, to avoid the awkward term "he/she," the terms "man" and "he" are to be interpreted not in the sense of the male gender, but either as "he/she" or in the sense of humanity as a whole (unless the situation obviously applies only to a person of the male gender).

Part I

One

The Tree
of Fire

Most Western men and women have lost much of the intense, emotional relationship which our ancestors had with fire. The threatening majesty of lightning, the magic of the spark, the flame, the light, the radiating heat, and the roar of living fire are becoming a thing of the past. A switch is flicked and light shines; steady, lifeless, and cold. Press a button and somewhere in a basement, hidden in a cabinet, controlled blue flames change water or gas into a source of instant heat for your house. Maybe (to set the mood, or as a prelude to sexual adventure) an atavistic

3

spark of subconscious memory makes you strike a match and light candles on the dinner table, or push the button which lights the gas in the phony logs of a fireplace.

I am one of the lucky ones; I am a child of the flame and the fire. I remember being led to bed by an aunt holding a flickering taper which cast eerie shadows on the wall. I sat and stared in awe at the roaring and crackling of living flames in my parents' gigantic, ancient fireplace, smelling the burning pine and oak, absorbing the heat into my body, and watching the slow, creeping combustion of the glowing embers.

Later in life, during World War II, I was pinned down by enemy fire in a house where a burning thatched roof was starting to collapse over my head. While living in Malibu, California, I assisted firefighters when a wall of flames came roaring down at us, followed shortly thereafter by an immense fire storm. In many places—but nowhere so grandly as in Africa—did I witness the majestic, fearful power of massive thunderstorms, with miles-long lightning bolts rending the sky above me. All this left me with an awareness of the living quality of fire and its capacity to awaken the awesome forces and energy of nature: creating, living, and burning, and then, as all life inevitably does, returning to ashes.

Lightning and fire are so closely related to life and procreation that modern scientists believe that the first physical creation of life on Earth took place when a bolt of lightning struck the primeval chemical "soup" which covered the face of our earth at that time—thus, literally, becoming the first "spark of life."

Fire, brought to man from the heavens by a bolt of lightning, and humanity's courage in taming this flame made an indelible impression upon our prehistoric ancestors. This is the essence of our oldest myths, the almost universal story of the Tree of Fire and Knowledge, a.k.a. the Tree of Life, the Burning Tree, the Burning Bush, etc.

No one knows how many millennia ago this event took place, changing life on Earth. The subconscious memory of this event has stayed with us, a memory of the very instant when people moved beyond being mere animals and began to gain control over their environment. The myth has been retold generation upon generation, half-forgotten here, embellished or adapted there. The same goes for the rituals performed to remind us of this event; they still exist, either in the form of religious ceremonies or as persistent customs. It was, and is, a story told by almost every clan.

The exact instant of this event is lost in the mists of time, but so many accounts in so many cultures tell us this same story, that I feel free to speculate on a possible scenario regarding the origin of this myth.

At some prehistoric moment, maybe on a cold evening around the time of the Winter Solstice, a fierce thunderstorm swept along a mountainside, scattering a small clan of human animals. They ran in fear as a blinding bolt of lightning lit up the forest, striking and igniting an ancient tree. While the rolling thunder echoed through the hills, they watched in awe as the flames snaked their way down the side of the tree and caused the branches to catch on fire.

Even from a distance they could feel the warm glow of the flames which lit up the night, and remembered how, in the past, Loki, the great snake of lightning, had stolen fire from the heavens and thrown it at the earth, creating a hell of flames that blackened hills and forest, killing all life in its path. This time, however, dampness prevented the fire from spreading beyond the tree. Suddenly a burning branch came crashing down in a rain of sparks, breaking into pieces, causing the onlookers to run to the safety of their cave.

One young female, however, held her ground; she chattered excitedly, then—fearfully and hesitantly—reached out to pick up a

A stylized picture of our oldest myth: the original gift of fire to man. The snake (lightning) has stolen the fire from the heavens to set the tree on fire and tempt the man (or traditionally, woman) to make use of this fiery fruit of knowledge. Man's fear of having broken the fire taboo led to his efforts of trying to return this fire by burning a tree, together with sacrificial gifts. It was the origin of man's burnt offerings, the Yule log, bonfires, and the Xmas tree.

Above: The terrible and awesome majesty of an electrical storm where—to the ancient beholder—fire was torn from the heavens and flung to earth. This was a fickle, random gift that could kill, destroy, or burn all, or as with the Tree of Fire, bestow a gift of light, warmth, and godly power. *Below left:* The rooster could protect against lightning, but also symbolized uncontrolled fires. (Not so long ago, Dutch farmers would say "the red rooster is present" when referring to a burning building.) This ceramic rooster with fiery comb and heart-shaped female sexual symbols is a tiny Portuguese good luck charm. The sexually aggressive rooster is seen as the bringer of new life, sex, and fertility. He is thus a symbol of all new life, and heralds the daily return (rebirth) of the sun, without which all would die (as seemed to happen each winter in northern lands). *Below right:* Golden rooster windvane on a fifteenth-century Protestant church in Holland. In pagan days, the rooster symbolized death/life, sexual reproduction, and fire. These forces were seen as one; the life force of nature. Lightning and fire would destroy all and bring death, followed by the rebirth of young greens and new life on a more fertile land, renewed by the fire's ashes. Thus, fire was also seen as a sexual, procreative force. The Christian Church retained the pagan superstitions and allowed the rooster on the church steeple to remain, now a symbol of the resurrection of Christ.

piece of the burning branch. Cautiously, holding it far from her body, she studied it, felt its warmth, and finally carried it to the entrance of the cave, where she danced around with it, then proudly laid it at the feet of the eldest male. He jumped back, terrified as much of the flame as of her sacrilegious act. Gaining confidence, she fed the flame with dry pieces of wood.

As a warm glow began to spread through the cave, and noticing that no heavenly bolt of lightning had punished the girl, the man and the rest of the clan moved somewhat closer. Fearful, but not wanting to be outdone by a mere girl, the man came closer still, then, after aggressively beating his chest, he gingerly picked up the branch. Nothing happened. Gaining courage, he started jumping around and excitedly waved the flaming brand at the terrified onlookers, who ran off to watch from a safe distance.

Emboldened by his newfound power and sexually aroused by the unseasonal warmth of the flames, the man reached for the young female, pulled her down next to the fire, and had sex with her.

This is a rather free rendition of the oldest myth of mankind. From the very beginning, man was afraid that, having received "stolen" fire (a fearful taboo)—and thus having acquired the first knowledge (science) of how to control nature—this represented an offense against the Great Spirit of Nature, an act that might bring nature's wrath upon him. In a sense he was right, for it opened a Pandora's box of troubles. After millions of years of slow evolution, it caused the sudden end of his animal paradise and set off a chain reaction which, to this day, continues at an explosive rate.

Man rejoiced in his newfound comfort and in the advantages it gave him over others, but he also realized that he had committed a "sacrilegious" invasion into a realm he could never quite control. In an effort to appease nature or the heavens, from where he felt his fire had been stolen, he placed sacrificial gifts on the branches of a similar tree and tried to set it on fire, thinking to return the fire together with his gifts of atonement. If the entire tree would not burn, he stuck flaming brands in the branches, or cut down the tree and burned it together with the sacrifices. He repeated this ritual yearly, as a gesture of thanks, fear, and appeasement; a ritual which he has performed, in one form or another, to this very day.

Realizing that there was little chance of soon obtaining fire in this same manner again, the shaman—later also known as Flamen, or "keeper of the flame"—ordered the clan's maidens to keep this fire burning permanently at all costs. Amazingly, thousands of years later, the Romans, who were by then very well-acquainted with the making of fire, still performed that same prehistoric ritual of "keeping the fire." Supervised by the Roman priest (still called Flamen), the Vestal Virgins still maintained the eternal fire, under penalty of death should they let it die.

Even though the use of fire by man was probably known 800,000 years ago by some, and the making of fire for some 100,000 years, there also still existed, as recently as the late nineteenth century, people (the Tasmanians) who did not know how to make fire. The myths of the origin of fire, as well as the ritual of its maintenance—passed on from generation to generation—are, consequently, both ancient as well as fairly recent. To this day, a flame is kept burning at all times in many churches, but the faithful usually do not know why, or else some new religious reason has been given, forgetting that similar flames burn in similar temples of almost all religions.

I mention this to show how long-lasting and strong such rituals and traditions can be. Once man's mind has been programmed by ritual, it behaves very much like a computer, and reprogramming is almost impossible; which is why we still celebrate the festival of the tree of fire, meaning that our Xmas tree has roots reaching back 100,000 to 800,000 years.

Fire, lightning, sexuality, and fertility have always been connected with each other, and with snake symbolism. Several of the messengers and guardians of God were, at times, depicted in snake form or as lightning: the Seraphim of the Babylonians, Hebrews, Canaanites, Amorites, and Hittites, as well as the fallen angel Lucifer (literally, the "light and iron-giver"). The story of the theft of fire from the heavens by a lightning-serpent who gave it to man exists in almost all cultures, from the Greek Prometheus to the Germanic Loki, to Indian legends, to the biblical story of the Garden of Eden, in which the snake (lightning) tempts Eve with the fruit (symbolic of fire and fertility) of the Tree of Knowledge (read: "Tree of Fire"; also called "Tree of Life").

In all the stories, once man has the knowledge of the use of fire (and learns how to make metals), he gains power and control over his environment and over life, but at the cost of forever leaving paradise and his idyllic, innocent (ignorant), animal state—the state in which he had existed in total harmony and symbiosis with the birth-life-death cycle of nature.

I never cease to be amazed at the incredible awareness of what we moderns so condescendingly call "primitive pagans," and at their deep insight into psychology, philosophy, sociology, and nature. Those people devised these myths, told these stories and passed them on orally, generation after generation, always warning man of the danger of lusting for power, excessive material wealth and the control of nature, warning against man's efforts to defy death, whenever he tried—in vain—to reach for immortality.

To this day, the tree of fire myth continues to teach us to wonder about nature; to be thankful for the miracles of fire, light, and knowledge, while reminding us to use our powers wisely, lovingly, and never selfishly. It warns us of the responsibility which has fallen upon us with the use and stewardship of this "stolen" knowledge (by now atomic!), by telling us of the terrible price man may have to pay for raping the land and dickering with nature, or, as they used to say, "for trying to step into the realm of the gods."

You may say, what can this old myth possibly have to do with our present-day Xmas tree? After all, the standard story is that Prince

Above: Fire: the gift Prometheus stole from the heavens and gave to man. This Greek mural is a perfect illustration of the ancient myth of the Tree of Fire. On the right, primitive man indicates the source of fire, allowing him to make tools and weapons to defend his freedom (indicated by the smith wearing the Liberty or Phrygian cap, worn in antiquity by slaves who had gained their liberty). The amorous young couple (extreme right) symbolizes the sexual creativity attributed to fire. *Below:* The task of the Roman Vestal Virgins was to keep the temple fire lit. If it ever did go out, the punishment was death; new fire was obtained from a lightning strike.

Above: An English Christmas tree of the late 1800s. *Below:* The lighting of the candles on the dark boughs of the evergreen. The warm glow of the flame and fire seem to trigger in man's subconscious the sense of awe experienced when we first received the gift of fire.

Albert, the husband of the British Queen Victoria, first brought the Xmas tree to England from his native Germany in 1840, where it —presumably—had been "invented" sometime in the sixteenth century. This story is usually substantiated by a 1521 German report and a painting from Strassburg of "the first known Xmas tree" (see color illustration). From England, the Xmas tree custom then, presumably, spread to the rest of the world.

A nice story, but incorrect and incomplete; the Xmas tree was mentioned in England in 1789, long before Prince Albert. When in the eighth century Saint Bonifacius came to convert the Nordic pagans, tree worship was still so popular that he felt he had to cut down the ancient holy tree dedicated to their god, Wodan. Later, in the Middle Ages, certain so-called mystery plays also featured decorated trees. Although the church compromised at first by adding holy Eucharistic wafers to the ornaments, they soon forbade the tree ritual altogether.

It only survived in certain pagan areas in the Baltics, too distant for control by the church. The Tree of Fire ceremony—as we mentioned earlier—has existed, in one form or another, since long before the birth of Jesus, ever since that day when man first stared in wonder at the gift of fire received from a burning tree. (It is probable that the account of the burning bush of Moses is connected with the Tree of Fire myth.)

Traditions of returning the "stolen" fire to god, together with sacrifices to make up for this "theft," exist among all people of Indo-European origin. It is usually connected with the New Year, Easter (originally the beginning of the year), or the Solstices (particularly the Winter Solstice, which is celebrated as Xmas).

It is important to be aware that we are dealing with what is basically one and the same kind of ritual and celebration, but a ritual which, for a variety of reasons, ended up being celebrated at widely different times by different tribes.

This was affected by:

1. The ups and downs and spread of the various religions—pagan as well as Christian.

2. The extent to which cultures adopted each other's rituals.

3. The degree of control leaders had over the people.

4. The problems of time-reckoning and of seasonal differences at different latitudes.

Two

Surviving Religion

For thousands of years, man's approach to religion has been a conflict between two concepts:

The Celebrant: The individual who personally tried to understand the meaning of life by loving and living it to the hilt, who watched the infinity of the star-studded skies, rejoiced about the daily return of the sun, celebrated the excitement of the hunt, the ecstasy of sex, and the miracle of birth, all the while feeling that he himself was part of the Life Force, which would joyfully reclaim him at the end of his days.

The Worshiper: One whose faith was based on fear and awe of a Force of infinite power and authority, a jealous god who had to be flattered, worshiped, appeased, and bargained with in the same manner that one had to deal with the old chief of the clan. Hence, one made deals with him to obtain favours, to be "saved," or to be forgiven for one's feelings of guilt for cultural or ritual trespasses (sin). But how could one make such deals? Well, as with the chief, by dealing with those who let it be known that only they knew the word of God and how to get through to him (often at a price).

The conflict between these two concepts still bedevils our present-day religions, with the fundamentalists as the standard-bearers of "Worship." Most religions, however, seem to contain elements of both concepts.

Religions commonly arise out of culture and environment; they spread with the culture, and are usually forced upon conquered populations. Even if the new culture becomes popular and the new religion takes hold, undercurrents of the old culture and religion continue to exist and tend to resurface as soon as the new power structure and its religion show signs of weakening.

Our customs and religions are imprinted on our minds: they are absorbed uncritically beginning in early childhood, and are further imprinted throughout the rest of our lives. Consequently, we rarely have a critical understanding of our own religion and its social, cultural, political, and economic effects. History shows that our position toward other religious points of view is only tolerant when their social, political, and economic aims coincide with those of our own culture. When aims conflict—as they did during the Inquisition and the Holocaust, as well as today in Northern Ireland, India, the Balkans, and the Middle East—religion will break its most basic precepts of peace and love to lash out murderously. To properly understand our past and present myths, we must understand how they were influenced by the cultures and religions forced upon the original population(s) by various invaders.

Above: Pachacamac, Peruvian horned god of volcanic fire, son of the Sun, nature god, random bringer of life and death, creator and destroyer, bringer of knowledge and art (compare to the Canary Islands figure below right). *Below left:* When the Roman Emperor Constantine the Great first favored Christianity and made the famous statement "In this sign I shall conquer," he did not do so out of idealistic love for Christian principles (he had his own mother executed), but used the early Christians as a core around which to gather the various religions of his time to give him a unified national Church with strong political power over the people. *Below right:* Small shamanic "devil" figure from the Canary Islands. This pagan, phallic good luck charm (now sold as an amusing, naughty tourist souvenir) is a benevolent but—as in all shamanic tradition—fickle, unpredictable figure representing fire, sexuality, and the random force of nature. In this case, he represents fire, not from lightning, but from the island's very active volcano. As with lightning, volcanic fire was of great help to man, but the volcano could also lead to his destruction.

Our present Western mythology cannot be properly understood unless we have some understanding of the pagan philosophy and practices from which it sprang, a concept which I, for the sake of convenience, will refer to as the "Olde Religion."[1]

The Pagan Olde Religion

There are, of course, no records of the thoughts of prehistoric man, but there is extensive proof that a pagan philosophy existed in Europe long before the coming of the Celtic and Nordic religions. We know, for instance, that, as early as 60,000 years ago, the Neanderthal custom was to bury the dead, after decorating the body with flowers. Traces of old nature philosophies and religions remained popular as an underground faith with the poor and even with some of the defeated aristocracy until long after the coming of the Christian Church. In remote areas of Europe, such remainders have existed right up to the twentieth century, and traces of it exist to this day (who these early people may have been shall be discussed later). The study of present-day hunter-gatherer tribes and societies, such as the Inuit (Eskimo) and American Indians, has also given us a better understanding of the old shamanic practices.

In studying philosophies and religions over long periods of time, we are faced with fluid, continuously-changing concepts. These concepts blend, reblend, and adopt each other's names, heroes, rituals, and traditions. They retreat temporarily with the onslaught of a new religion, then reappear when the new religion and its political regime weaken. Few have gone "underground" for as long—and resurfaced as tenaciously and frequently—as the Olde Religion, which is actually more of a way of life and a relationship with nature than a religion. This tradition is symbolized throughout ancient Europe and the Mediterranean shores by its horned, shamanic protagonists.

---

1. *This should not be confused with the modern groups which began to spring up in the late nineteenth century.*

In its purest, earliest form, we are probably dealing, as I said, not so much with a religion, as with a philosophy of celebration, man's way of relating to the forces of nature and to the mystery of creation. Early man believed that everything around him—animal, mineral, or vegetable—was part of his existence; part of his consciousness. Every event had a cause, every action resulted in a reaction, since the entire world was in balance. In primitive life there was no concept of right or wrong, and, consequently, no such thing as sin. There was creation and there was destruction, with life and time suddenly existing between them. It can be compared to an electric circuit with a plus and a minus pole. Nothing happens until you short-circuit these two poles, then—zap! Like life, energy, sparks, light, heat, and time are born and go on existing until all the energy is used up, whereupon time and the seeming reality of existence ends, or is dead.

A modern parable may further illustrate this seeming contradiction:

Man is like a candle which is manufactured (created), but remains without purpose until it comes to life by being lit; it "lives" as long as it burns. When the wax is used up, the light "dies." It is this process of destruction which allows life to exist. The flame and the light it sheds for that short while are pure energy and are the main purpose of its life.[2]

Thus, the forces of creation must fade into those of death and destruction, to maintain life and allow it to fulfill its purpose. In nature, there exists no right and wrong, no good and evil.

There were—and are—useful clan taboos, of course, but these did not deal with sin in its absolute and religious sense. They were originally established to protect the well-being of the clan (similar to American traffic rules which require drivers to drive on the righthand side of the street, while in England the rule is the opposite; there the taboo is against driving on the right. Breaking such

---

2. *Compare Zen and the Yin and Yang concepts of Eastern philosophy.*

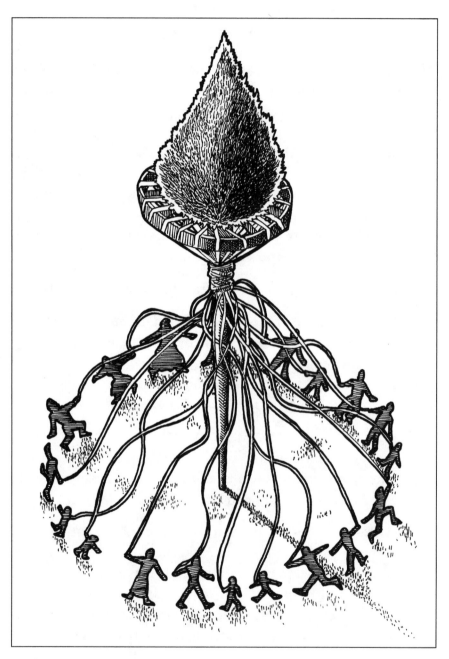

The Yule log and the Maypole were some of the variations on the Burning Tree. After the sometimes-elaborate celebrations, both were originally burned with offerings.

taboos may cause physical danger and punishment, but it certainly does not make it a moral sin in either country).

To the pagan, sex—the meeting between the Yin and the Yang—led to life. Consequently, the sex organs and procreation were celebrated joyously at feasts; like nudity, they were never a source of embarrassment, shame, or a reason for concealment. Since the hunter-gatherer's way of life could only sustain a small number of clan members, there was always the danger of inbreeding, thus interclan sexual orgies at the great hunting feasts helped to enrich the gene pool.

In later years, all this, of course, became anathema to the authoritarian Christian Church, which equated pagan concepts of creation and destruction with their own moral, religious separation between right and wrong. Their most severe punishment was reserved for those who sinned by having trouble understanding and accepting the Church's definition of these concepts. Oddly, Christian society, with Alice-in-Wonderland logic, would override its own religious commandments about sin and absolute right and wrong whenever it suited its own purposes.

The commandment "Thou shalt not kill," for instance, suggests that killing a fellow human being is morally wrong and sinful. If caught doing so, you may yourself be killed, or punished severely and dishonored. If, however, the authorities decide to put you in a uniform and order you to go into a foreign country to kill as many fellow human beings as possible, then wrong suddenly becomes right; killing becomes your righteous, patriotic duty, for which you will be honoured and rewarded with medals. Not only that, you will now be wrong and severely punished if you refuse to follow the order to kill. This leads to the conclusion that the concept of right and wrong is not a God-given absolute, but is, like traffic rules, a set of human rules dictated, or agreed upon, to fit society's power-politics and the social needs of the moment.

Another difference was that these early pagans did not share our later anthropomorphic concepts of gods-in-the-image-of-man.

Fickle, king-like gods, far above us on a mountaintop or in Heaven, observing us, making deals with us, and sitting in conscious judgement of us, using (and abusing) their awesome powers over us—this concept was made more palatable by the early Christians by changing it into that of a more loving Father figure. Compared to those often rather bizarre concepts, early man's concept was simple. Like the Native American, he believed that everything, animate or inanimate—including himself—was part of the Great Force of Nature, a concept akin to the modern environmental idea of Gaia, the living earth.

Early Western man felt very close to the trees of his great forests. Anyone who has spent time in a majestic old forest, be it pine or deciduous, knows that eerie feeling of sensing ancient life all around oneself, a life that exists at a majestic, sedate tempo, in a time frame far slower than ours. Speed up time with a special camera and the movement of branches and leaves furling and unfurling, following the sun, appears as gracefully alive as a herd of mustangs galloping across a plain. As we now also know, trees in a great forest are not just individual trees, but tend to interconnect through the network of their roots.

Man thought that these trees harbored the spirits of ancient life. The shaman acted out this communion between man and nature. In a theatrical impersonation of natural forces, he spoke for the spirit of the forest and its wild animals, and he spoke for man, the hunter. In essence, he mediated between them, establishing the mystic love, respect, and thanks of the hunter for his prey; for he and the prey were part of one and the same body of nature. This attitude allowed both man and his prey to exist, as well as the trees in the forest which sheltered him and supplied his needs. For modern city man these are not easy concepts to grasp, yet any old-fashioned farmer who needs to slaughter his pet pig for food will understand.

Like all pre-Christian religions, the Olde Religion relied upon animal and occasional human sacrifices; even the Romans performed religious human sacrifices until the third century B.C. To date, many rulers and governments have sanctioned mass killings for the sake of religion or cultural, tribal, or national purity. Such genocide may also take place for revenge, or even fun and excitement. Sadly, every day of the week, television and films "entertain" us with killings, both real and fictional (the latter often portrayed in a frighteningly realistic manner), and the violence still fascinates, titillates, and excites too many of us—and our children.

Of course, not everything was perfect in the early pagan world. Things were relatively peaceful as long as it was a world of simple, communal hunter-gatherers, but as agriculture and animal hus-bandry developed and overpopulation reduced the hunting grounds, greed became a new factor. Also, not every shaman was altruistic—some abused their power, and not every witch always used his or her ancient knowledge and herbs to cure. They could also poison opponents, or supply poison for arrows to help defend the clan against the new, warlike tribes which were invading the land, forcing them to withdraw and hide in the forests, marshes, and mountain ranges.

The Coming of the Gods

New, terrifying, tall, powerful men from the heart of Europe invaded the old pagan world of small hunter-gatherers. These men from the new Bronze and Iron Age, the ancestors of modern Western man, were nomadic and highly mobile, with carts and cavalry. They raised and raided cattle and did the same to these little hunter-gatherers as their Christian descendants did, 2000 years later, to Native Americans. These men brought with them new concepts of gods: mythical, godly middlemen who were a strange blend of nature spirits and ancient folk heroes, chiefs, or founding fathers. These gods were now recognized as the con-trollers of nature and man. To the original inhabitants, these gods were, like the new aristocracy, fickle and dangerous figures, with reputations for raping, killing, and robbing one another as well as the human population.

To survive, one had to make deals with these gods, in much the same manner as one had to deal with the new rulers. Among the better-liked of these were the solar deities (usually the son of a greater chief god), who each day brought warmth and light to man's world, then slept during the night. In the far north this god died in winter, but was resurrected in spring. Remnants of this concept persisted as late as the seventeenth century, where the French king Louis XIV insisted on portraying himself as the god-like Roi Soleil (Solar King), great benefactor of France.

It may, at this time, be important to remember that man initially created gods in his own image, not the other way around, as the Judeo-Christian religions would have us believe. If you think about it, it is a very bizarre and quite improbable idea that the supreme force of the universe would select one particular, messy little mammal as the exclusive physical reflection of its own being.

Certain celebrated shamanic performers may inadvertently have helped in giving an anthropological image to the forces of nature and themselves become early gods, such as the early horned and masked Germanic god Frey who, like Pan, was usually depicted with an erect penis and a flute; both were fertility gods known for the defloration of virgins.

These new conquerors and their gods were nomadic big-game hunters and raisers of cattle. Symbiosis with the land, communal sharing, and equal rights were now replaced by a male-dominated, warlike culture, expressing the right of the strongest—the ruling class with their ruling gods. These in turn were replaced by new rulers and new gods of the even-stronger Germanic/Nordic tribes, as well as by the still stronger and better-disciplined Romans. This pattern of aggression, exploitation, and growth has continued until today. This macho-male concept involved perpetual growth, taking without asking, war, and forceful readjustment of the environment to fulfill people's needs and wishes, rather than a life in balance with nature. Conquerors behaved the same way everywhere—in Persia, Greece, Rome, Germany. It was the birth of modern Western civilization.

This drawing of a Dutch waffle iron (1733), with pagan and Christian symbols, is a late example of the bizarre blend of the Christian, Nordic, and Olde religions that existed in remote rural areas.

Between two Tree of Life symbols we see the Christian cross under the INRI sign (meaning Jesus of Nazareth, King of the Jews), the tools of crucifixion, the dice with which the Roman soldiers gambled to win Jesus' robe, and the coins of Judas' betrayal. To the right, we see the crucifixion ladder, a scourge, and a besom (broom), as well as the rooster, the Christianized pagan symbol of lightning, fire, virility, and rebirth. To the left, the symbols can be considered both Christian and Germanic: the spear (which pierced both Odin's and Jesus' side) and an 8-shape on a rod (either the sponge that quenched both Odin's and Jesus' thirst or the 8-shaped *Odal*, emblem of Odin).

The column, the cross, and the ladder all symbolize the Tree of Life, Yggdrasil the world tree, the resurrection, and the Omphal axis of the world (the world phallus of Pan; of "All"). Again, this symbolizes the three religions, with the trident on the columns as a special symbol of Herne/Pan. The church later condemned the trident as a satanic symbol.

The new religions and cultures had much in common and overlapped; they combined vaguely-remembered nature gods with deified heroes and resurrecting solar gods. These were all faiths of warrior races who invaded and oppressed the earlier, weaker, and smaller races, whose only choices were to either become serfs or slaves or to hide in marshes, on distant islands, in the forests, or in inaccessible mountain valleys.

Celtic Culture and Religion

Few details of the early Celtic religion are known. The Celts seem to have had a multitude of anthropomorphic gods and mother goddesses: deified heroic leaders, minor nature gods and animals, as well as others obviously acquired during their nomadic roamings. Some were very old, such as the horned god Cernunnos, who seems to have been derived from the shamanic Herne/Pan figure. The Celts had a mysterious body of priests—the Druids—who acted as intermediaries with some of their gods. They had holy groves and lakes and performed human and animal sacrifices. They also had a solar god. It is, at times, quite difficult to keep the Celtic culture and religion apart from that of the closely-related Nordic/Germanic people.

Nordic/Germanic Culture and Religion

In many ways, this belief system closely resembled and overlapped the Celtic—and, later, the Greco-Roman—religion, showing resemblances resulting from their mutual Indo-European past and even with the later Christian faith. In the third song of the Icelandic *Eddas,* the god Wodan/Odin was "hung on a tree" (Yggdrasil), suffered there for days, was stabbed by a spear in his side and, presumably, was a great benefactor of mankind who taught man the art of runic writing. Yggdrasil was the shamanic tree, source of life and knowledge, which stood in Midgaard (middle garden), inhabited by early man and Loki's fire serpent. There are distinct similarities here to Christ on the cross and the Garden of Eden.

Greco-Roman Culture and Religion

This included the same Indo-European solar-god background as the Nordic/Germanic religion, along with a pantheistic assembly of older and foreign gods from conquered nations. Among these was Herne, our ancient shaman, now known as Pan and reduced to the role of a minor forest spirit.

Christian/Roman Religion

In part, this religion was a continuation of the religious establishment of the Romans, but with a restructured theology established by Emperor Constantine at the Council of Nicea (A.D. 325). For his new (political) theology, the Emperor used the then-minor Christian religion as the framework, combining it with old Roman traditions and elements of various other prevalent religions, such as the resurrecting solar god Mithras, while also allowing elements of the popular Mediterranean Mother-Goddess-and-Child cults (such as Isis and her son Horus, the divine child) to be incorporated into his new, paternalistic religion.

This pattern of transforming popular pagan deities and rituals continued into the early Middle Ages. Old pagan feasts were changed so as to honor the Christian saint on whose day the particular pagan feast had customarily been celebrated. With the end of the Middle Ages and the coming of the Inquisition, the Church had made a major effort to forcibly destroy any surviving vestiges of pagan culture or religion; it did not, however, ever succeed in eradicating them completely.

The Protestant Reformation

In certain areas, the Reformation caused the collapse of the Roman Church's authority. Old pagan customs resurfaced during this time, having spread from pockets of paganism that had survived in isolated areas, such as the Dutch Wadden Islands, the Bavarian mountains, and countries such as Lithuania which had always remained pagan. As soon, however, as the Protestants were firmly in power, they too did all they could to destroy these pagan remnants, but were no more successful in doing so than the Catholics had been.

It seems highly peculiar that, unlike several other religions, the Judeo-Christian religion chose to portray the gift of fire, light, and knowledge as evil. The Lightning-Serpent, Loki, Prometheus, and Lucifer should have been seen as man's friends, but instead were portrayed as Satanic opponents of God, while humanity was called sinful for trying to gain knowledge. This was typical of monopolistic ancient priesthoods, which tried to keep outsiders from competing in matters of power and knowledge. They required a safe-and-obedient status quo, and tried to destroy all (even men like Jesus of Nazareth) who encouraged people to think creatively and independently, autonomous of the control of Synod or Curia.[3]

---

3. *Curia: used in the sense of the ruling class of the Vatican, the ultra-conservative governing body through which the pope leads the Roman Catholic Church.*

Three

The Reckoning of Time

When dealing with autumn and winter feasts, we notice that similar feasts occur in different areas at totally different times, some as early as late summer, others later, on Saint Martin's, Saint Thomas', Saint Nicholas', or Saint Peter's Day, Xmas, New Year's, or as late as March. Why? In order to unravel this confusion, we must first understand how time reckoning and calendars worked—then and now—and how frequently changes in such reckoning were made in some countries, while not in others. Secondly, we must remember that autumn started much later in the south of France, for instance, than in Norway or in central Russia.

To early man, time was as confusing a concept as today's fourth dimension is to the average person. Time was understood vaguely as "then," "now," and "later," or was based on simple solar or lunar events, such as "at sunrise," "high noon," or "sunset." Future dates could not be established very far ahead of time and were at best "two days after the next full moon," or set rather vaguely, as "after the snows have melted." Establishing more precise, long-term dates was the exclusive magical/mystical monopoly of their scientists (the shamans and priests), a secret art these individuals had learned to master surprisingly well.

The next time you see someone laying out cards to foretell the future, remember that those playing cards at one time probably were a cut-up, early calendar (possibly of Egyptian origin), with the fifty-two cards each representing one of the four monthly lunar phases (about one week). The Houses represented the four seasons, as well as—in descending order of importance—the four social classes. Hearts (the symbol of the female genitals) stood for the nobility (who still had the right to any woman); Diamonds for the military caste (represented on old cards as soldiers carrying spears with diamond shaped points); Clubs were the clergy (originally carrying Celtic-type crosses); Spades stood for the peasants (carrying spades). The color red traditionally symbolized power (social, military, and sexual power), versus black for submission (both spiritual and physical).

Part of the confusion in time reckoning throughout history is due to the introduction of calendars which, although supposed to make things easier, actually made them more complicated. After thousands of years of accurate lunar and solar time reckoning by shamans and priests of pagan religions (whose calculations, of course, differed, depending upon their latitude), a yearly calendar system was introduced by the Romans and the Roman-Christian church, as a system of uniform date and time-keeping, accurate in

Above: Representative figures for Spades, Hearts, and Clubs. *Below left:* The Five of Diamonds. *Below right:* The closer to the equator, the more accurately a sundial operates. In the northern hemisphere, due to the shorter days in winter and longer days in summer, the sundial daylight hours are longer in summer than in winter. A standard length for hours only came about with the invention of mechanical clocks.

any part of the Roman Empire. This was a system which any army officer could interpret for himself, without the benefit of priest or shaman. Unfortunately, this early calendar turned out to be quite inaccurate over longer periods of time, causing celebrations (now set on the new calendar dates) to move out of sync with the seasons and the previous lunar and solar timing. Remember that the length of the year—even in our modern calendar with its leap years—is still minutes longer than its 365 days and has to be readjusted regularly.

Today, few people realize that, in western Europe, the calendar was changed in 1582 (in England only in 1752). At this time, the beginning of the year was changed not only by two months, from March 1st to January 1st, but also, later, reset by 11 days. This meant that May 1st suddenly became May 12th! Before that time, dates had been set by the old-style Julian calendar of 46 B.C.

This new Gregorian calendar was decreed by Pope Gregorius to correct the (by now major) errors of the old calendar, thus establishing our present system. This explains why the names of the months of September, October, November, and December (which in Latin mean the seventh, eighth, ninth, and tenth months) have, in a most confusing manner, become the ninth, tenth, eleventh, and twelfth months. Add to this that the Celts used to start the new year on what is now November 1st, and the Germans on November 11th, and you can see how the same celebration might end up on completely different calender dates. This is especially true if, as in some rural areas, popular tradition stuck to the old solar dating, while others switched to the modern calendar. Members of the Eastern churches insisted on sticking to the ancient Julian calendar until 1923.

One holiday still set according to solar and lunar events is Easter, held on the first Sunday after the first full moon following the first day of spring (approximately the Vernal Equinox, the day in spring when the length of the night is equal to the length of the day). That is why the celebration of Easter falls on a different calendar date each year.

Over the centuries, the above-mentioned changes and the accumulated errors in different calendars caused the Winter Solstice to no longer be in sync with the feasts. Our present Christmas Day on December 25th is three days late. In Russia, it's held on January 6th, while Holland starts its winter celebration around December 6th (Saint Nicholas' Day). None of these festivals any longer match the true Winter Solstice, which presently occurs on December 22nd.

To further confuse matters, each day used to "begin" at sunset (as is still customary in the Jewish religion) instead of at midnight, which is the reason why we still celebrate Saint Nicholas' Eve, Christmas Eve, New Year's Eve, etc. on what is considered to be the evening of the day before the official holiday.

Seasonal Differences

Depending upon how far north the clans moved, the date for the latest possible harvest came earlier in the year (and so, consequently, did the date for the slaughter of much of the cattle, since herds had to be culled due to shortage of winter fodder). Harvest/slaughter festivals, which in southern areas might have coincided with the Winter Solstice in late December, might, in the north, have to be held as early as Saint Marten's Day (November 11th) or Saint Nicholas' Day (December 6th). Other changes were caused by the advent of improved farming methods in certain areas. The resulting more abundant supply of fodder allowed the cattle to be fed a few months longer, which pushed the slaughter date later into the year.

You can see how, due to all these changes, the same closely-related traditional pagan rituals and feasts ended up being celebrated months apart. Take Xmas, Thanksgiving, Saint Martin's Day, Saint Nicholas' Day, Halloween, and New Year's Day—all, at one time, were the same celebration. The American Pilgrim Fathers, for instance, refused to celebrate their fall/winter feast on Christmas Day, which they considered to be a heathen and Papist (Catholic) feast. So they moved their feast earlier, to the end of November, where it had been in earlier times. We must also remember that the weather in that part of the world was far more severe, and thus a harvest/slaughter feast would have to be earlier than in England.

I hope all this has given you a better understanding of time, calendars, and date setting in the past. We can now return to our Xmas tree and its origins, as well as to the mysterious shamanic figure which, after thousands of years, ended up as the modern Santa Claus.

Four

The Ancient
Memory

No one knows the exact date upon which man first began to use fire. It may have been as long ago as 100,000 years ago. The use of fire was probably discovered in many different places at different times, but with the exception of areas with volcanic fire, it was always as a result of lightning. The myth and the rituals of lightning and the burning tree, which kept alive the memory of this event in man's mind, may be as old as one thousand centuries.

Whether man had to move because of the onslaught of the ice age or whether, equipped with fire, he left the warm, subtropical areas of his origin for the more northern parts of Europe and Asia, the winters brought a frightening time in which the length of the day gradually became shorter. Trees shed their leaves, and cold, snow, and ice seemed to indicate that the sun and all life around man was dying. It was a time of fear—fear that evil forces were eating or destroying the life-giving warmth and light of the great fireball in the sky. Was it a punishment for man because of his sin—the theft of fire—that evil forces of darkness would now destroy the sun (similar to the way in which we today fear man's misuse of science as a possible cause of the hole in the ozone layer)? After all, man had only been able to move to these colder northern regions because of his possession of fire and clothing. Once there—particularly during the last ice age—the winters must have been terrifying, and many must have died in the cold and snow before learning how to adapt.

To them, it must have seemed a vital ritual to appease the gods by returning the stolen fire, together with sacrificial offerings, by hanging sacrificial gifts in the branches of a holy tree, then setting the whole thing on fire. Like all magic, if it helped, fine; if it didn't, no harm had been done. Everyone had a roaring good time performing the ritual, and you could always eat and drink what was left of the sacrificial gifts. The latter was an important point, since in those ancient days (and still today), these religious rituals were not just solemn occasions, but times of joyous, lusty carousing, with much eating, drinking, lovemaking, and scaring-away of evil spirits.

Along with this, a special meaning was attached to ancient trees and evergreens, such as ivy, holly, and mistletoe, which all brought forth fruit in winter.

These plants were used to decorate the native huts during the winter feasts, since they were seen as the continuing spirit of life and as heralding the return of the sun. In a letter written in 601, Pope Gregory the Great refers to the natives' custom of building shrines of branches and greens around their pagan temples. He advises his bishops to allow the people to continue doing so around such temples as had been changed into Christian churches, in order to help win the hearts and minds of these pagans for Christianity. It is possible that the Jewish custom at Succoth was also originally derived from similar pagan customs.

Mistletoe was sacred to the Greeks and Romans. It was supposed to originate when lightning hit trees (without causing them to burn) and represented life energy (read "sexual energy"). The Celts called this mistletoe the "Thunder-Besom" (from the besom, or broom, an ancient sexual symbol of both the male and female organs). The Germanic tribes believed that all who passed under the mistletoe were kissed (blessed by sexual power) by Freya, their goddess of fertility. Today, 2000 years later, we still perform minor fertility rites under the mistletoe.

Not only was mistletoe seen as a symbolic fruit of lightning, fire, and sexual energy; because of this sexuality, it was also seen as a symbol of peace. Since the tribal expression of this sexual energy led to the stealing of females of other clans, and this, in turn, to intermarriage between clans, it tended to reduce warfare. This is illustrated in the famous historical account of the Roman rape of the Sabine maidens, who, in the next war between the Sabines and Rome, threw themselves between the combatants, holding up their new offspring, pleading—successfully—that their Roman husbands, as well as their Sabine fathers and brothers, would stop killing one another.

Whether in spring as the Maypole, or in fall or winter as the Yule log or Xmas tree, the tradition of the burning tree continued throughout the generations, together with its customs of sacrifices (which in time became gifts to the church, and later, to one's friends and loved ones), feasting, dancing, and fertility rites.

In spring, a specially-chosen Maypole tree is cut, the lower branches are removed, and it is raised with a (solar) wheel attached to the top. It is then lit and burned down, after which a guard is posted to save and protect the fire. It is an excellent

Above: Certain ancient trees (mostly oaks) were sacred to the pagans. We know little about why they were held sacred, only that they seem to have been rallying points for the pagan resistance to the invading Christian power. Wherever the Church and its kings and barons gained force, these holy trees were forcibly cut down. *Below left:* Stealing a kiss under the mistletoe. The Xmas season allowed a certain sexual permissiveness. *Below right:* As one of the evergreens which blooms in midwinter, the holly, with its shiny red berries, was symbolic of the continuation of life when all else lay dormant. It carried with it a promise of the return of the sun and new life.

Above: This early twentieth-century illustration shows a Druidic, pagan Father Christmas with the shamanic joker as his helper. The figures are surrounded by Xmas greenery. **Below:** "Holy" mistletoe was a symbol of fertility and survival of life through winter; it fruits in mid-winter. Its presence allowed wild behavior that was not tolerated at other times. It is here seen in an illustration from *The Pickwick Papers* by Charles Dickens.

"Christmas for Ever!"

This late-nineteenth-century Santa is pictured with holly and mistletoe.

example of the ancient return of the fire ceremony, even including the prayer for the return of the sun by its inclusion of the solar wheel. The guard is an ancient reminder of the days when fire from lightning was irreplaceable and had to be fed and guarded at all times (study the Roman Vestal Virgins for an example of this). Remaining pieces of wood from the fire are kept in the home and are believed to protect the home from being struck by lightning.

The solar wheel is related to early Yule/Xmas celebrations and combines a variety of symbolic meanings. It is the Sun Wheel, with its spokes dividing the year into seasons, showing the movement of time. When set on fire and rolled down the mountainside, it symbolized fire and the return of the sun. In Northern Europe, this custom still exists in remote valleys. There you will also find the flaming sun wheel symbol as a decoration on thousands of wood-carvings, cakes, cookie molds, bedsteads, and embroiderings.

Today, in the areas where the Maypole ceremony is still practiced, the pole is rarely burned, except in a few ancient villages, such as Denekamp in the Netherlands. Although the villagers are unaware of the meaning of the ceremony, at Easter the Maypole is ceremoniously brought in in the same manner as is done with the Yule log in Nordic countries. It is erected in the village square, and a small barrel, as well as a wagon wheel (the old solar emblem), are attached to the very top. A generation or so ago, the barrel contained tar, which, when lit, would drip down the pole and set the whole thing on fire from top to bottom. This is now considered too messy and polluting, so the barrel is filled with wood shavings which burn with a rain of sparks. You may wonder why people did not simply burn down a tree, but you must realize that in the cold, damp north European countries, it was virtually impossible to set fire to a fresh, green tree.

In the seventeenth century, the American Puritans (the Pilgrims, the founding fathers of the city of Plymouth) expressed horror at seeing the identical, happy, pagan ceremony being performed by neighboring English settlers. The Puritans attacked them, cut down their Maypole, and banished their leader.

To the Greeks and the Celtic Druids, the oak (that notorious drawer of lightning) was the holy tree of fire; to Nordic tribes, it was the fir (fire) tree or the ash. Wherever we investigate old traditions, we find ritual connections between lightning, burning trees, burning logs, holy candles, and great bonfires (with fertility rites involving jumping over those fires). In pagan days, the tree was supposed to contain the spirit of life, which was released in the form of fire when the tree was hit by lightning. Later, the branches of the Xmas tree were supposed to protect against lightning, as were remaining pieces of the Yule log or the Easter candle. The Druids are supposed to have tied gilded apples to the tree as a symbol of fire, in honor of the god Wodan (after whom our Wednesday is still named. More about this god's connection with Saint Nicholas later on).

According to Frazer's *Golden Bough,* certain African tribes believed that, when lightning strikes a tree—setting it on fire—all fires must be extinguished and new fire must be lit from the stricken tree, while in parts of England and other places, no fire or matches may be taken out of the house on Xmas. Similarly, the North American Natchez tribe had a taboo stating that if a fire went out, it could only be relit with the fire from a temple or with pure fire obtained from a tree hit by lightning. In the Persian myth, it is Ahriman who, "springing like a snake (lightning) out of the sky down to earth," creates man and arranges to have him obtain fire from a burning tree, and teaches him how to cook as well! The Nordic sagas known as the *Eddas* also contain an account of a burning tree.

The lightning/fire myth is so universal that even the South African Bushman tribe has a myth which tells about man losing his idyllic existence in their equivalent of paradise, when he obtains fire from lightning.

On December 25th, the Greeks had their Helia (from *helios,* the sun) winter feasts assuring the return of the sun, and shortly thereafter, another festival called the Basilinda. The Romans had similar periods of feasting called the Saturnalia and Kalendea, in which they not only exchanged gifts, but also decorated trees, or, in the cities, decorated their homes and wrapped posts with green branches, all trimmed with gifts and lights. There was great sexual freedom; roles were reversed, masters served slaves, and there were mock kings called "Lords of Misrule," very similar to our carnival traditions and closely connected with the medieval "boy bishops" of the Saint Nicholas festivities. There were still older customs— very much frowned upon by the early Church—involving men dressing up in hides, animal masks, and women's clothes; similar customs were also known in ancient Greece.

In Northern Europe there existed another version of the burning tree, the Yule log, which was originally an entire tree, and later a huge log. It was dragged into the village or home to be ritually burned at Xmas time, after which its ashes were saved, since these were supposed to have strong fertility powers (wood ashes do make good fertilizer), as well as to protect against lightning. For that reason, in some areas, pieces of the Yule log are still saved to be burned during thunderstorms to protect the home.

Although the burning of the Yule log is best known as a Nordic-Germanic tradition, it actually is an Indo-European-Aryan ritual from a much earlier time, also practiced by the Persians. The origin of the word "Yule" is uncertain; some think it is connected with the old Saxon word for wheel, *hweol,* and that cutting and rolling the Yule log led to the invention of the wheel. This seems incorrect. The word "Yule" still exists in Dutch as *joel* or *jol,* meaning "loud, fun, rambunctious partying," related to the Gothic name for the month of December, *juleiss,* meaning the month of celebrations and partying. After all, the flames of the burning wood also represented the sexual, creative nature—the life force of fertility.

There are a few places where huge fires are still lit, in some instances with a flame that may only be made by rubbing wood together, or better still (according to the custom), stolen from somewhere! The fire has the power of fertility: people dance and

Above: Raising the Maypole/burning tree in the Dutch village of Denekamp, the only village where the Maypole is still burned. Note the broom-like appearance. *Below left:* The traditional solar wheel. *Below right:* This picture shows how deeply ingrained the tradition and subconscious memory of the pagan burning tree still is. This seven-foot tall candelabrum in the shape of a tree was recently designed for the non-denominational Velsen crematorium in the Netherlands.

Above: A sixteenth-century German painting of the oldest known Xmas tree.
Below: This French picture shows the combination of tree worship and the
adoration of Saint Nicholas; an obvious effort by the Church to Christianize
pagan tree worship and the veneration of other traditional pagan figures. Such
practices still existed in many parts of Europe into the early twentieth century.

jump over the flames, and there is much partying and sexual activity (as in many of our Xmas and New Year's parties today). Cattle used to be driven over the glowing coals, and the fertilizing ashes were cast over fields.

Even in countries where the Catholic Church had maintained full control since early Roman times, the worship of the Tree of Fire survived, as can be seen in old customs such as the French *Buche de Noel* (literally, "Yule log"): a special pastry in the shape of a log, served around Christmas and the New Year.

By the way, *Noel*—the French name for Christmas—comes from *natalis,* the Latin word for birthday. In ancient Rome, this birthday referred to the December 25th Winter Solstice celebration of the rebirth of the Unconquered Sun (Sol Invictus). The Church later conveniently changed this to the birthday of Christ, although, admittedly, the actual birthdate of Jesus is unknown.

In the eighth century, when the first missionaries, Willibrod and Bonifacius, came to convert the Frisians and Germans, they felt it necessary to forcibly destroy the latter's holy trees. For centuries thereafter, the Church tried to eradicate any form of tree and Maypole worship, but was never entirely successful in doing so, particularly since they could not effectively control all the outlying areas where paganism survived. When, with the rise of the Reformation, the power of the Roman Catholic Church dwindled in these now-Protestant areas, tree worship resurfaced in the form of Xmas trees, Yule logs, and Maypole celebrations.

There exists a sixteenth-century German painting on parchment (see illustration on page 45) with the oldest known Xmas tree picture. It came out during the revolutionary period when the Reformation had just broken the power of the Catholic Church, when remnants of long-suppressed pagan habits had a chance to resurface.

The fact that the villagers at the bottom of the picture are drawn much smaller indicates that the others are larger-than-life mythical figures: first the musician leading the parade, then the man with the whip pointing down (to hell?) with his right index finger, followed by a man carrying the oak Xmas tree with reddish, shiny metallic ornaments (symbolic of fire). Many forget that, particularly in countries with milder climates, the original tree of fire was the oak, the holy Germanic tree.

The papal-looking figure on horseback, reminiscent of the Dutch Sinterklaas, actually represents a pagan figure. Unlike the Pope's three crowns, he only has two on his tiara, the crowns of spiritual and of temporal power, making him a mythical, pagan priest-king. In his hand he holds what is probably a pomander (an amulet-like device holding fragrant substances), used either for blessing or for exorcising evil spirits; both very shamanic activities. In this case, he seems to be blessing the tree. His coat—with the green vines—indicates that he is a nature spirit; I suspect a blend of the shaman/king and the Germanic god Wodan, both ancestors of Santa Claus.

Such pagan revivals did not last long. More puritanical Protestant forces soon gained control and suppressed rituals such as these. Not until the late eighteenth century, with the coming of the Enlightenment and the French Revolution, was the power of the Church sufficiently reduced to, once again, allow a resurgence of such pagan traditions which had secretly survived in inaccessible mountain villages or isolated islands, as seen in a nineteenth-century French engraving (see illustration on page 45) of a hollow, holy oak tree (obviously hit by lightning at one time) in which a figure of Saint Nicholas has been installed. Two young women are praying at the foot of the tree, either to get pregnant or to find a husband. This is a very late example of tree worship, combining its powers of fertility with Saint Nicholas as the patron saint of barren young women.

The Xmas tree reappeared as a pine tree in the enlightened, late eighteenth century. Why as a pine tree and not an oak?

The oak which, centuries earlier, had been the subject of tree worship in Germanic countries, was becoming scarce, and was still too closely remembered by the Church as having been associated with

Germanic pagan rituals. The pine tree, however, which in the colder mountain areas of Germany had long been the tree for such ancient ceremonies, was cheap and plentiful, burned well, and, being straight, was more easily transported. According to an old German legend, when the old pagan Holy Oak was cut down by the missionaries, a small pine tree arose from its roots. It became the Xmas tree of choice.

Part II

Five

The Shaman:
Santa's Earliest Ancestor

Where does the modern Santa Claus come from? Around the end of the nineteenth century, his cult spread from America to England, and, during World War II, to the rest of the world. Santa was not—as some Americans believe—invented by Clement C. Moore in 1823 for his poem "A Visit from Saint Nicholas," with the famous opening words, "'Twas the night before Christmas and all through the house …"

Santa was re-born in America in another way. In 1626, a ship with settlers from the Netherlands reached America and founded the Dutch colony of New Amsterdam. The figure-head on their ship was that of Saint Nicholas, the patron saint of sailors. These Dutch colonists brought their winter holiday customs with them, which involved the good Saint Nicholas (known in Dutch as "Sinter Claes," which was later anglicized as "Santa Claus"). A mere thirty-eight years later, the colony was ceded to England and became New York. Soon the Dutch seemed to disappear, absorbed by a much larger British population.

One hundred and fifty years later, the Dutch were but a memory; only a few of their names—such as Roosevelt and van Buren—remained, and some vague memories of their quaint customs. When American essayist Washington Irving mentioned the old Dutch Santa Claus legend in his *Knickerbocker History of New York,* it inspired Clement C. Moore to write a very inaccurate poem (with fictional reindeer replacing the traditional white horse), in which he re-introduced Santa Claus and described him as an elf. Boyd, his first illustrator, ignored this and drew a strange little Dutchman smoking a stubby clay pipe (see illustration on page 54). Forty years later, this poem was illustrated for Harper's magazine by the famous cartoonist Thomas Nast. Not having the vaguest idea what Moore's elf was supposed to look like, the Bavarian-born Nast drew Santa Claus as the winter holiday figure he remembered from the mountain villages in his Bavarian Alps; a rather scary, less-than-friendly gnome (see illustration on page 54), dressed in animal skins and carrying a short broom-like rod with which to threaten girls and boys.

Over the years, Nast's Santa became a bit friendlier, until, in 1931, the Coca-Cola Company decided that they wanted to increase their sales to children. The law at the time did not allow advertisements showing children drinking Coca-Cola,[1] so how

---

1. *In its early days, it was said that Coca-Cola used coca (a narcotic plant from which cocaine is made) leaves in its recipe. Consequently, the drinking of Coke by children was frowned upon and advertising of Coke for children was not allowed. By 1931, Coca-Cola had changed its recipe, but the law was still on the books.*

about showing a friendlier Santa Claus, relaxing with a Coke served to him by children? The artist Haddon Sundblom was assigned to come up with a new, more commercial Santa. Instead of Moore's elf or Nast's grumpy gnome, Sundblom came up with the large, jolly fellow in the well-known, bright red suit with white fur trim (the Coca-Cola colors). In World War II, this reborn Madison Avenue[2] Santa marched to victory alongside Coca-Cola, as both conquered the world.

The truth, however, is that this American Santa Claus only represents the tip of a very ancient iceberg. Santa existed long before the New Amsterdam Dutch, Clement Moore, Thomas Nast, and Coca-Cola—his roots go back tens of thousands of years. The search for Santa's origin constitutes a genuine detective story, leading back to prehistoric times and man's earliest concepts of religion.

Disentangling the roots of a mythological character to find its original ancestry is no easy task, since over the centuries, these roots have cross-connected and interwoven into an incestuous tangle. The story of one tribe's hero may, for instance, have been taken over by another tribe who attached it to their own tribal hero. A thousand years later, a new culture absorbed the two stories—which by now, may seem to be unrelated—and added them to the biography of yet another god, saint, or hero, acceptable to that new culture. The progression from prehistoric shaman to the Santa Claus of modern commercialism is just such an intricate story.

The Shaman

Man's earliest effort at understanding and communing with the Mystery of Life was through the example and guidance of a shaman or medicine-man/woman. Such people had two tasks:

---

2. *Madison Avenue: A New York City street where many advertising agencies are located, hence, symbolic of the advertising world.*

Above: Boyd's Dutchman/Santa Claus. *Below:* Nast's Bavarian "Dark Helper," known there as Knecht Ruprecht. He is the old Herne/Pan figure, still scary and in furs, but no longer sporting horns or displaying genitals.

Above: Over the years, Santa Claus became more friendly and less frightening, as shown in this illustration by Thomas Nast. ***Below right:*** This Victorian American Santa has hung his animal-skin fur coat on the rack and looks pretty modern and civilized. Only the Jack-in-the-Box gives a sly hint of his scary, fickle, sexual, shamanic nature (at the time, "Jack-in-the-Box" was a slang term to indicate copulation).

"For Santa"

The modern international Santa Claus, drawn by Haddon Sundblom for the Coca-Cola Company.

one was that of spiritual guide and teacher for the clan, showing them how to stay in harmony with the forces of nature around them, interpreting and acting out that mystical bond. The shaman's other function was material; being the earliest scientist, he was the Keeper of the Flame (Flamen)—the cook, the keeper of all knowledge, astronomer, mathematician, time-keeper, judge, historian, and bard. The shaman taught stories by song and by rote, as was still done thousands of years later by bards like Homer; the shaman taught the ritual dances of the hunt, of war, of reproduction, birth, life, and death.

To achieve this, the shaman used sound, music, dancing, mimicry, masks, make-up, costumes, and art, as well as fire, sex, and violence. To these things were added—when speech became common—singing and storytelling. All this was done in much the same manner as it is done today, in what we call "showbiz." Thus, the shaman was also the producer, artist, and media-coordinator of his day; the clan's poet/philosopher who had memorized the sum of the tribe's knowledge. The *Odyssey* and the *Iliad,* as well as the Old Testament, are written versions of such ancient, accumulated oral philosophy, history, and knowledge.

At celebrations, the shaman would appear masked, as the physical embodiment of the spirit of nature. Sometimes he did this in a trance, under the influence of drugs or hemp vapours (like the Greek Oracle at Delphi). While in this state, some shamans might have believed that they, at that moment, actually became (channeled) the voice of the nature spirit. This type of shaman still exists and is known to us from Siberian natives and from Native North and South Americans. Aspects of shamanism still exist in various religions, as in the Catholic Church, such as when the Pope speaks *ex-cathedra* (from the seat), presumably speaking infallibly in the name of his god (incense having replaced the hashish fumes of yore).

As one nears the Winter Solstice, the days become shorter and the nights longer. In the far north, the sun may vanish completely and darkness overtake the land, until, on the day after the solstice, the

The long-lasting and universal nature of the Herne/Pan shamanic figure is indicated by this variation on an illustration from East Russia, originally drawn by a member of an eighteenth-century Dutch expedition. Note the animal skins and the claws on the shaman's feet.

Above: This English horned dance photograph is remarkable in that it also shows a man (right foreground) wearing a skirt—the old shamanic custom of occasional cross-dressing. *Below:* The Herne dance at Abbot's Bromley, England (originally performed at Xmas), is an ancient shamanic ritual, at one time meant to magically assure a good hunt and the fertility of the herds.

days grow longer again, the sun reappears and rises higher in the sky, while the nights get shorter. All this is followed by a general reawakening; in nature, the more abundant sunlight warms the earth and causes the resurrection of life and the greening of the land. At the time of the Summer Solstice this action is, of course, reversed.

It is obvious that if a shaman could learn the mystery of how to calculate the exact times of these solstices, he could then greatly enhance his position by "miraculously" predicting the exact day of the return of the sun. He might stage this ceremony, along with the return of the gift of fire sacrifices, whereupon—lo and behold—the evil of darkness was placated and exorcised, and, to the amazement of the uninitiated, the days would immediately start growing longer. The sun god had been saved or resurrected! The initiate could learn when to expect the miracle of the solstice by watching the changing shadows cast by tall stones or poles, then marking the exact position of the shadows on the ground. Soon the land abounded with temples featuring such early calendars and other astronomical marking stones. Thus the early science of astronomy, calculation, and calendars was abused to falsely give the shaman personal, "magical" power with which he could gain social power and enrich himself. It meant that these individuals stopped being shamans and became the founders of the first priesthoods or secret brotherhoods, who carefully guarded their "magic" knowledge and surrounded it with ritual and mumbo-jumbo to make it harder for outsiders to learn their secrets. Similar secret lodges later became popular with others, such as masons, smiths, and doctors. (To this day, doctors seem to pride themselves on writing prescriptions in a kind of illegible code that only a trained pharmacist can decipher.)

Such religiously-guarded mysteries were kept far from the common man, but the holders of physical power, the warrior kings, soon realized that, by working in partnership with the priesthood and thus combining physical with scientific and emotional power, they could gain absolute power. This was the origin of the Priest/Kings. Such traditions last long. Her Majesty the Queen of

England is, for instance, not only queen of the realm, but also head of the Church of England.

The discovery of means of broader dissemination of knowledge to the public—first through eloquent speech, followed by the inventions of writing, printing, and cheap paper, and shown today by the explosive rise in new means of communication—has always resulted in revolutionary efforts against exploitation of these methods by the priestly/educational establishment and its ruling classes. These same power-brokers would retaliate with efforts by church and state to control these new media in order to retain their monopolies on power, knowledge, and mind control.

Another unfortunate effect befell the early shamans. Certain particularly wise, talented, and inspiring shamans—remembered by later generations—were themselves made into mythical heroes and finally into demi-gods. Remembered symbolic performances became transformed into "reality" after the death of the performer, a common event in many religions. Siddhartha, an Indian prince, became Gautama Buddha. The Nazarene carpenter/rabbinical teacher Jesus was seen as the expected Saviour, the Christ, and became the mythical hero of Christianity—half man, through his mother, and half son of God. On a modern, less-exalted level, after her early death, Marilyn Monroe—a tragic, sensuous young actress—is remembered and made into a modern love goddess; a twentieth-century Venus. In somewhat the same manner, the memory of one of these early hero-shamans may have become the demi-god/spirit Herne/Pan, performed yearly by new shamans in sexy, anthropomorphic reruns of the original performances to audiences of frightened, but happily aroused, fans.

The original shamans, however, were not priests and certainly not gods, but respected, knowledgeable members of the clans, who "felt it and did it" by putting on the masks and garments, or else were asked to do so by the clan. Anyone familiar with the Saint Nicholas ritual, as still performed around December in every city of the Netherlands, cannot help but be aware of the fact that the

Above: Horned shamanic masks continued to exist in Europe into the twentieth century, ending up as scary children's toys (center foreground). *Below:* This was one of the last known shamanic masks in England. It disappeared at the end of the nineteenth century, when it was stolen from the house of its Dorset owners. Its exact age is unknown. Note the similarity between the mask and the "toy" above.

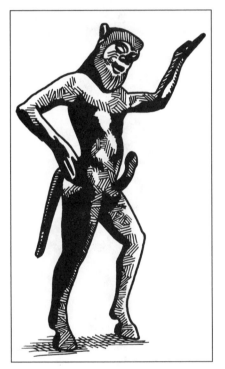

Above: The shaman dances. In this 10,000-year-old mural, the Herne/Pan shaman dances behind a group of (reindeer?) does, and uses a bow to play a kind of string instrument. It seems to be a symbolic fertility ritual (note the erect penis) to magically increase the growth of the herd. Until quite recently, it was customary to chase the cattle through the glowing ashes of the Xmas bonfire to produce the same effect, since ashes from such a "holy" fire were supposed to guarantee fertility. *Below left:* A drawing of a Greek statue of Pan. *Below right:* This ancient Greek vase shows a version of the Herne/Pan shaman with erect penis.

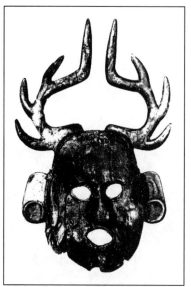

Above: This Dordogne shaman (detail of illustration on page 63) is the earliest known picture of the masked, dancing shaman. Note the similarities to the Ariege shaman and the North American shamanic mask below. This figure could be called the first Santa Claus. The difference in horns is due to the clan. Clans originating in colder, northern areas hunted deer or reindeer; clans from warmer, more forested areas hunted the aurochs, and thus took the bull as their symbol of nature and protection. *Below left:* A sixteenth-century North American mask, with horns nearly identical to those on the figure at right. *Below right:* The horned shaman, from a cave painting in Ariege, France, of about 10,000 B.C.

person appearing and dressed as Sinterklaas (the Dutch equivalent of Santa Claus) is treated with great (nowadays mock) respect, even by the city's mayor or the queen! Performing this shamanic role is still considered to be a distinct honor.

Like simple, early man, children have always been totally at ease with symbolic impersonations; they put on a mask and become the scary monster, or whatever the mask represents to them and their friends. At times, even modern adults behave this way. Dress a man as a doctor, minister, or general, and he is treated with reverence, without any question as to whether he deserves it. A fascinating side effect, however, is that individuals often seem to grow into the part, acting worthier and more responsible than they were before.

From prehistoric times well into the Middle Ages, the clan's most respected shaman seems to have been called *Duyvel* (then a respectable title, not synonymous with Satan). Other wise women and men who acted as scientists, doctors, midwives, and herbalists were called witches. All were held in high esteem until as late as the sixteenth century. When appearing as the spirit of nature, the shaman usually wore a mask, horns, and animal pelts; he was Herne/Pan—the Horned One—the leader of the wild hunt. He danced, made music, and appeared with an erect penis to symbolize procreation. The American Museum of Natural History has Native American masks with staghorns, which are almost identical to those shown on the cave drawings of Dordogne (see illustration).

It is interesting to note how common similar displays of sexual prowess still were in the Middle Ages, particularly for men of the ruling classes. In the 1450s, during the reign of the English king Edward IV, noblemen used to wear a pair of hose unconnected at the top, which—since they wore no underwear—left their genitals bare.

Over this they wore a very short, belted tunic which was either split open in front, or so short as to teasingly display the male member. Since not all men were well-endowed, they improved upon their display by wearing the so-called braquette, or codpiece ("cod" was a slang word for penis); a greatly enlarged and sturdily erect, padded, glove-like cover for the male genitals. This provocative device was exposed proudly between the garments and can be seen in a variety of paintings, some as late as that of Henry VIII in the sixteenth century.

Some small pieces of fourteenth-century Dutch jewelry show how at ease the population then was with sexually explicit symbols. This particular item (see illustration on page 68) shows the erect Tree of Life set inside a decorative vagina-shaped arbor, along with two little penis-shaped figures. The "veil" in the tree is a traditional symbol of life and death, and of male/female interaction. It also stands for "truth hidden from the uninitiated." It was a fertility amulet/gift for a young woman.

Until the sixteenth century, sexually transmitted diseases were either non-existent or of minor importance in the north and west of Europe. Consequently, the people had always enjoyed sexual freedom, particularly at the great celebrations. However, as with AIDS today, an epidemic of syphilis—a hitherto unknown disease—brought this happy sexual freedom to a sudden stop and allowed the Church to proclaim this disease as the wrath of God against such permissive pagan practices.

The Herne/Pan shaman usually carried a fire brand, a musical instrument, and the besom (the Greco-Roman version of this became the Thyrsus rod). This broom-like rod was, until the end of the eighteenth century, a symbol of the male/female sex organs; hence "broomstick-marriages"—marriages not sanctioned by the church, but by jumping over the broom, as in certain old gypsy and back-country marriage ceremonies, still well within memory. Most of us are, of course, aware that this same broom was also part of the witches' ceremonies. What the cross was to Christians and what Thor's hammer had been for the Germanic religion, the besom/broom and the tree continued to be for the Olde Religion of the pagans: symbols of their belief. In illustrations as late as the

Above: The English King Henry VIII, a descendant of the Plantagenets, proudly displays his braque, or codpiece. (The Plantagenets, like many old noble families, had roots in the fertility cult of the Olde Religion.) Had Henry lived a century earlier, he would have flaunted the real thing in the same manner. Such exhibitionism was reserved for nobility. Together with the massive costume, it promoted the image of the king as not only the ruler, but also the top procreator; the powerful "bull" of the nation. *Below:* A well-endowed warrior of the 1500s.

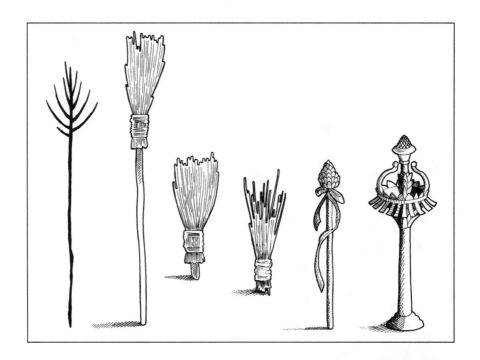

Above: The besom was a holy fertility symbol of the Olde Religion of very ancient origin. Left to right: the oldest known image of the besom, from a cave painting at El Castillo, Spain. (Anthopologist Leroi-Gourhan interpreted it as "a stylized male/female symbol.") Two traditional besoms, or witch's brooms. Saint Nicholas' and the Dark Helper's broom/switch. The Thyrsus, the Greco-Roman equivalent of the besom. The prize besom of Shaftesbury, a Church processional object. *Below left:* This sketch of an early fifteenth-century small silver brooch from the Netherlands features the Tree of Life festooned with the Veil, and phallic figures and symbols. *Below right:* This Santa Jack-in-the-Box by Nast still brandishes the shamanic broom.

twentieth century, the short version of this same broom-like rod is still brandished by Santa Claus or by his Dark Helper.

Modern people live according to vestiges of 10,000-year-old pagan rituals and myths. Think of the 5000-year-old story of Noah's Ark; toy arks are sold in stores today. Equally odd is that in spite of all the anti-pagan actions of the Church, the Western nations continue to use the names of 2000-year-old Germanic and Greco-Roman pagan gods and forgotten pagan festivals to identify their days of the week and names of the months.

Pagan Day Names

English	French/Latin
Sunday for Dies Solis, the day of Sol Invictus; the Iranian Mithraist, resurrecting solar god	Dimanche, Dies Dominica; the "Lord's" day
Monday for the Moon goddess	Lundi for Luna
Tuesday for Tyr (Norse), or Tiwz, Germanic war god	Mardi for Mars, Roman war god
Wednesday for the god Wodan or Odin (Norse)	Mercredi for Mercurius
Thursday for Thor or Donar, god of thunder	Jeudi for Jovis/Jupiter
Friday for Frey and his twin sister Freya, god and goddess of sex and marriage; the Nordic adaptation of Herne/Pan	Vendredi for Venus, Roman goddess of love
Saturday for Saturnus, ancient Roman god of agriculture	Samedi; origin uncertain (derived from Saturnus?)

Pagan Month Names

January, after the ancient Roman god Januarius.

February, after the Roman feast of purification, Februarius.

March, after the Roman god of war, Mars.

April, the Roman month Aprilis (exact meaning uncertain).

May, month of the feast of the ancient Roman goddess Maia.

June, after the Roman goddess Juno.

July, after the Roman "god"/emperor Julius Caesar.

August, after the Roman "god"/emperor Augustus.

(September, October, November, and December were the seventh, eighth, ninth, and tenth months on the old calendar.)

*When
Santa
Was a
Shaman*

Six

The Cross
and the Broom

When the Christian Church first appeared in Gaul and Britain, it did so as the state religion of the declining Roman Empire and was, in many ways, a continuation of the previous, easy-going Roman religion. The Celtic and Germanic warlords saw the pagan Roman religion as little more than a name change of old gods: Thor became Jupiter; Freya became Isis or Venus; and Wodan could be seen as identical to Mercury or other resurrecting solar gods, such as Apollo or Mithras. Christianity seemed like yet another name change: Jupiter was now called God,

Apollo and Mithras changed to Jesus, and the Virgin Mary easily replaced the mother goddess Isis. After all, these were all Indo-European cultures with similar traditions of Father, Mother, and resurrecting solar Son gods.

It was a different story when, some 500 years later, the Roman-Christian Church moved into areas where the population had never been under the Roman yoke. Here, the Church had to deal with back-country populations who had been resisting their overlords for centuries. The missionaries (as missionaries have of necessity been throughout history) were also known to be the eyes and ears of the invading kings and emperors who, at this time, were competing Christianized Celtic and Gothic warlords. They now ruled "by the Grace of God" (and the Church), conquering and converting, with the cross in one hand and the sword in the other. They unfortunately used Christianity, not so much to gain the hearts and souls of the people, as to make it easier to exploit their servitude and enforce obedience.

It was a situation very similar to the European colonization of North and South America in the seventeenth, eighteenth, and nineteenth centuries. The teaching of the Christian Church that you may have to suffer through this vale of tears called life, but that—if obedient—you will later, after your death, be rewarded with glory, salvation, and equality in the hereafter, was quite handy in encouraging the conquered populations to remain docile and to submit to serfdom and the yoke of their new rulers. A few wealthy opportunists converted rapidly, but the poorer population, as well as some of the old nobility, accepted only a token veneer of Christianity, while quietly sticking to their own customs. Many a new village priest or bishop saw nothing wrong with saying a Christian mass while still officiating for the Olde Religion (similar to the relationship between Christianity and Voodoo in modern Haiti).

Consequently, the besom and the shamanic Herne the Hunter were not just the archaic emblems of their ancestors, but living symbols of freedom and resistance against the conquering alien aristocracy and their cross.

Who, exactly, were these early inhabitants, these vanished ancestors of whom so little is remembered?

The "Little People"

Some 10,000 or more years ago, at the edges of the great British and continental forests, and probably throughout Europe and around the Mediterranean, there existed neolithic, hunter-gatherer populations who lived in close harmony with nature and their environment. It is believed that men and women held fairly equal positions in these tribes.

In their function as gatherers and as the keepers of 10,000 years of cumulative knowledge of nature, certain of their shamans (both men and women) were known as "Witches," individuals who were highly-respected for their knowledge of herbs, as midwives, and as healers, and who were also feared and employed for their knowledge of herbal poisons. In those days, the name "Witch" seems to have been a term of respect rather than of dislike. Up until the days of Cromwell and his Puritans, for instance, almost every large British country household had one of these "Witches" on its staff, employed as a midwife, healer, herbalist, and at times, as a caster of magical spells.

The traditions of these people (as with the early Greeks and today's Gypsies) were oral; their trading with outsiders was based on the ancient barter system, still practiced in recent times between forest dwellers and men from the plains. In this system, goods are left at a pre-arranged spot. While the seller hides, the buyer comes, takes such goods as he likes, leaves his own goods in payment, and then disappears. The seller then emerges from his hiding place to pick up the payment goods. (This method of trade was still common with the Pygmies and other African tribes in the late nineteenth century.) The practice is also clearly described in English stories of dealings between so-called "faeries" or "elves"

Above: A genteel nineteenth-century illustration of the kidnapping of the Sabine maidens by the Roman warriors. The stealing of women from other tribes was still a necessity deriving from the days when small, inbred clans desperately needed fresh genes. *Below left:* With figures such as these, the Church tried to demonize the Olde Religion, depicting it as bizarre, satanic, and evil. This figure incorporated the horned shamanic mask, the bisexual aspects, the male fertility trident, and other pagan symbols. *Below right:* The hanging of witches. The final genocide of the Little People and the rest of the descendants of the early neolithic population (by the warlike Celts and Germanic invaders) was achieved by the destruction of the Olde Religion and its witches and shamans.

Above: Size comparison between the Germanic/Celtic invaders and the earlier population of Little People. Although the races and tribes are now mixed, these two sizes are still commonly found among European Nordics and the Mediterranean populations. In earlier times, these contrasts were more pronounced. *Below:* A fanciful rendition of our Little People, seen here as a hairy, wild man and woman, based on a late-medieval illustration. Their sodhut is familiar to archaeologists. According to *A History of Witchcraft* by Jeffrey B. Russell, these people were associated with witchcraft and the Wild Hunt.

and their Celtic and Nordic conquerors, it being mentioned that strict honesty and fairness was always observed.

Like most hunter-gatherers, these gentle people tended to be considerably smaller of stature and more delicately built than the large, beef-fed Celtic and Germanic warriors who invaded their lands (see illustration). We must remember that, in those days, the human gene pool was far less mixed than today. Tall tribes like the Frisians were even taller than they are now, with many of them well over 6'4"(1.93 meters), while people from tribes that were short of stature would seem quite small to us today. Visitors to European museums are often astounded to see that uniforms and ladies' dresses of the previous centuries would nicely fit today's twelve-year-olds.

The little we know about these hunter-gatherers reminds us of more recent, once nomadic, northern tribes, such as the Native North Americans, the Eskimo (Inuit), and the Lapps. Like so many small, inbred clans, they seem to have been very much at ease sexually. Compare the Eskimo custom (still remembered) of encouraging the women to have sex with visiting strangers, a custom which would result in the improvement of the small tribe's gene pool. Like certain Native North American tribes of the nineteenth century, they may also have been openly bisexual (which was one way to, when needed, keep the clan's population small enough to survive). On the other hand, sexual orgies at the great hunt gathering of the clans helped to enlarge the gene pool and increase the health of the next generation.

Such free and open sexual behavior horrified the Roman-Christian Church, and later, Cromwell's Puritans, who both saw in this kind of behavior the doings of Satan. In its efforts to destroy this Olde Religion, the Church taught that their shamans and witches were servants of Satan, the theological adversary of the Christian God. The image of the aroused Duyvel-shaman, dressed up as the spirit of the hunt, adorned with horns and animal skins, was, from then on, used by the Church to portray Satan. This is why we now think of the, once-respected, shamanic titles of "Witch" and "Duyvel" as aspects of the Evil One.

There were, however, far more important (political) reasons than sex why the Christian Church and the occupation force's ruling class wanted to blacken the image of the Olde Religion. It was, after all, the defiant religion of the oppressed. The "Little People" had resisted the earlier Celtic and German invaders; now their descendants continued to do so against Rome. To the poor, native population whose land and game had been appropriated by alien kings and their bishops, the spirit of Herne (backed by his outlaws' arrows) still roamed freely through the forests and hills, to, as in the past, hunt wherever it pleased, thumbing its nose at this new aristocracy with their slaves and serfs (for an example, examine the closely-related Robin Hood legend).

This conflict simmered for centuries. On a different level, it also represented the conflict between the worship-oriented, male-dominated, authoritarian, aggressive power of the Cross, and the celebrating, male/female principle of sexual and personal freedom and quiet resistance, symbolized by the Broom. As late as the sixteenth century, Dutch naval units did not carry the cross on their sails (as did the Spaniards), but went into battle with the besom in the mast,[1] not just to sweep their enemies from the seas, but to express their spirit of freedom from the Catholic kings.

Even within the ranks of the Church itself, the power of the broom remained strong with certain followers of the teachings of Jesus (whose own teachings so often spoke up for humanity, love, and the celebration of life). In the Middle Ages, many wonderful priests, monks, and religious people combined the best of both the Olde and the Christian religion within their vocations.

Meanwhile, in the name of Christ, the Vatican instigated a series of genocidal crusades and persecutions against such pagan and heretic Christian factions; crusades in which hundreds of thousands of

---

1. *Even today, Dutch skippers use pagan symbols, as when they tie a green, leafy branch in the mast to indicate a birth, Christmas, or other event.*

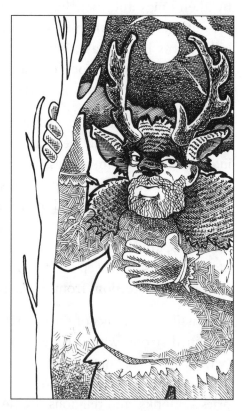

Above: Fourteenth-century monks throw up their hands in horror at the antics of the Herne/Pan shaman and his masked clan figures, or mummers. Five hundred years later, Shakespeare romanticized the mummers' rituals in *A Midsummer Night's Dream. Below left:* Cernunnos. Hardly anything is known about the Celtic religion, but we do know that the Celts had a horned god called Cernunnos. It is probable, but far from certain, that this god was derived from the shamanic Herne/Pan spirit of the hunt. *Below right:* In Shakespeare's *Merry Wives of Windsor,* Falstaff hides in the forest, near Herne's holy oak, disguised as Herne the Hunter.

Above: Cernunnos, the horned shaman, from *Legend: The Arthurian Tarot* by Anna-Marie Ferguson. *Below left:* These beings from a tarot card (La Diablo, from the *Tarot de Marseille,* 1761) are based on the hermaphroditic, shamanic, horned Herne/Pan; here caricatured to make the ancient shamanic title Duyvel synonomous with the Christian Satan. *Below right:* The shamanic Herne/Pan, after a fifteenth-century tarot card, complete with sex symbol trident and satanized with bird feet.

Above: The Christmas masque, a medieval version of the Great Feast. Note the horns around the fireplace and other pagan symbols. *Below:* Santa's "great-grandfather," the Herne/Pan shaman in post-Shakespearean England. This figure is known as Robin Goodfellow or Puck. He is still horned, clad in fur, holding fire, dancing to music, and shown with an erect penis. He also brandishes that ancient European sex symbol, the witch's broom.

men, women, and children died horrible deaths, many by being burned alive. To date, the Vatican has never officially admitted that these genocidal actions were erroneous.[2]

Many of these heretics were Aryan Christians who had disobeyed the Vatican's orders by translating the gospel from Latin and allowing services to be held in their own languages (thus allowing the common man to become aware of Jesus's revolutionary social teachings). These dissidents also disagreed about the Trinity, believing that Jesus was not himself God, but separately inspired (a prophet). Such theological decisions about what was right and what was wrong thinking were the closely-guarded monopoly of the Christian Church, as was knowledge. Any layman found dabbling too much with knowledge was in constant danger of being labeled a heretic.

In spite of the teachings of Jesus—including his belief that the law was there for man, and not man for the law (Mark 2 and 3)—the Christian religion had, with Emperor Constantine, become a fundamentalist religion, intent upon eliminating any form of criticism and maintaining its own absolute rule and that of its kings and emperors. A typical example of the arrogance of the latter was Charlemagne, who humbly prefaced his personal letters with: "In the name of the Father, the Son and the Holy Ghost, I, Charles, the Illustrious and August, crowned by God, Emperor of Peace and Protector of the Realm of Rome, and by the Grace of God King of the Franks; greetings …" It is rather obvious that God and his Church were supposed to be there for the emperor, and not the other way around. A way of thinking that, sadly, is still alive and well in many countries.

It is fascinating to see how the fundamentalists managed to change even the meaning of a word. The original meaning of the

---

2. *The Vatican rarely admits its errors and oversights. Only in 1994, fifty years after the fact, did the Vatican finally formally condemn the Nazi Holocaust.*

word "heresy," for instance, was nothing more than "another choice" or "a different point of view." For having a different point of view,[3] was the Christian Church, at that time, willing to murder a million people? (Even today, some religious fundamentalists are so opposed to "freedom of choice" that they are prepared to murder a doctor in order to discourage women from exercising their legal right to terminate an unwanted pregnancy, or to condemn the writer Salman Rushdie to death for openly daring to criticize certain aspects of his own faith.) Was it surprising that so many of the medieval pagans only converted to Christianity at swordpoint?

The remaining Little People were forced to retreat, first to the heart of the ancient forests, then to marshes and inaccessible mountain areas, until, in time—like the Bushmen, Veddas, and Pygmies—they faded away, partly destroyed, partly absorbed by their conquerors. Since they used mostly wooden tools, few clues remain of their existence, other than their tiny stone-tipped arrows (the so-called "elf darts") and hundreds of myths and legends. Thanks to recent research, numerous historical references have been found in sixteenth- and seventeenth-century documents and records, as well as inscriptions on grave stones, all attesting to their existence and intermarriage with villagers from normal-sized tribes.[4]

Being expert archers and woodsmen, they could, in their forest-green clothes, blend into the forest, appearing and disappearing at a moment's notice and, with their small bows and (sometimes poisoned) arrows, they could silently dispatch their enemies in the defense of their lands. All this instilled a superstitious fear in their

3. *Today's Christian fundamentalists give a similar spin on the word "humanism," which is simply a philosophy that asserts the dignity and worth of humankind and its capacity for self-realization through reason, while rejecting supernaturalism.*

4. *Dr. Margaret A. Murray's controversial books* The Witch Cult in Western Europe *and* The God of the Witches *make for fascinating reading on this subject.*

The Little People among the Romans. Once you are aware that the Little People were simply members of cultures absorbed by their conquerors, it is surprising how often you find them depicted with normal-sized citizens. Here, the Roman emperor Marcus Aurelius is seen performing a sacrifice, aided by two Little People. The flute player's features are radically different from those of the Romans around him and are reminiscent of the features of Pan. Although the Romans were short compared to the Celts and the Germans, they are still more than a head taller than the Little People here.

overlords, leading the latter to the belief that the Little People were endowed with supernatural powers; myths which these Little People—like the African Pygmies and later the Gypsies—were only too happy to help perpetuate.

Other hints about their existence can be found in legends of faeries, elves, gnomes, and trolls, and in stories such as those of Robin Hood. They seem to have been similar to, and certainly culturally related to, the Lapps of Scandinavia. It is interesting that their clothing is often described either as forest green with pointed caps, or—as in folkloric accounts of their witches—as identical to costumes worn by nineteenth-century Lapps.

Up until the sixteenth century, faeries and elves were mentioned as normal, smallish, rather "hippie-ish" creatures of a different culture, but no more alien than, say, Gypsies. Only in Shakespeare's play *A Midsummer Night's Dream* were they first depicted as ethereal (although still normal-sized) creatures.[5] These beings only became ridiculous, tiny-winged creatures in the fantasies of the late eighteenth- and nineteenth-century Victorian romantic writers and illustrators. Victorians also bypassed the social mores of the day by depicting pagan semi-sexual or nude goings-on, but linking such antics to cherubs, tiny faeries, and elves.

These small people traded and intermarried with the villagers on occasion, but like today's Gypsies, they had their own customs and lived in, or near the edge of, the forest. Like Gypsies and Jews, they were falsely accused of all kinds of crimes, including child-stealing and ritual killings, but compared to their warlike oppressors, they probably were rather gentle and peaceful. They liked dancing, used the bow and the reed flute as musical instruments, and believed in an all-encompassing spirit of nature, the forest, and the hunt. Hence, one of that spirit's many names: Pan (meaning "all encompassing"). It represented both birth and

---

5. *Even in Shakespeare's* Merry Wives of Windsor, *Mistress Anne Page—a normal, full-grown young woman—is mistaken for a faery woman.*

death, creation and destruction, the Yin and the Yang, with life flowing harmoniously between.

To better understand this philosophical concept, we must temporarily abandon our traditional Christian beliefs which tend to equate God with a Father image enthroned in the heavens, ruling the universe and passing judgement on us mortals. Their nature spirit was not anthropomorphic (in the image of man) at all. It represented the sense of being part of the whole of nature—more than that, it was the intrinsic feeling that every storm that blows, every tree that falls, every breath taken, every animal killed, every word spoken, and every action performed, in a very real sense, affects the entire world around us, either positively or negatively, for now and forever after.

Consequently, it meant that every action or event had to be balanced with a counter-action, every kill in the hunt had to be apologized and made up for, to maintain not only the balance of nature, but also the balance within the tribe and within the individual's own life and soul. It meant that every individual was related to and partly responsible for everything else; a concept surprisingly close to today's ecological Gaia concept.[6]

The role of the shaman at first differed considerably from that of a priest acting as God's agent. The shaman, while performing his function and dressed in a symbolic manner, had a visionary experience and temporarily became Herne/Pan (the spirit of us, the forest, and all of nature around us) in the sense that he—to use a present popular word—"channeled" this spirit through his being. Consequently, we read of individuals meeting and talking with Herne/Pan in person, similar to a present-day child meeting and talking with Santa Claus. To the child, that person is not just representing Santa, he really *is* Santa!

---

6. *Science also confirms that any action causes a corresponding reaction in the balance of the universe. This may not be noticed by humans, only because the change may be so minute on the grand scale of things as to not always be recorded. Larger changes, however, such as solar flares, are very noticeable (as a result of their effect on Earth's magnetic field).*

A shaman might be one of the clan's leaders, a wise man or woman, or a guru living as a hermit in the forest. In early days, each clan probably had a shaman of its own, appearing masked and dressed as that particular clan's totem animal.[7] The tradition of the gathering of such clan shamans in their animal masks is shown in ancient manuscripts and still carried out in Christmas "mummer" parades, such as the one in Philadelphia.

Since many leaders and kings wanted to see themselves as divine priest-kings, some of them (such as Alexander the Great and Moses) were depicted with shamanic horns. Children fathered by the shaman during religious orgies may also have been considered to have special powers, which may have led to the bizarre concept of classical heroes (and even historical kings and emperors) who had presumably been fathered by Zeus in union with an earthly maiden.

The Christian Gospels show traces of this same tradition in the story of the Annunciation, when the angel Gabriel announces to the young virgin Mary that God's "Holy Spirit shall be upon her," causing her to become pregnant and have a son who would be both God and man: the hero of future Christianity. This was one reason why Saint Paul's version of Christianity fit so easily into the Roman/Hellenistic way of thinking, yet was totally unacceptable to the Hebrews who, at that time, did not believe in an anthropomorphic God,[8] and to whom this kind of miscegenation was blasphemous.

As mentioned earlier, the shamanic Herne/Pan went by many names, depending upon the tribe and era, but he was most often portrayed as dark, furry, or wearing animal skins, with antlers or horns, and—up to the seventeenth century—with an erect penis.

---

7. *Compare this to our modern ideas of Russia as the bear and America as the eagle, or think of British regiments with bearskin hats, animal mascots, and drum majors with panther skins over their uniforms.*

8. *At the beginning of the first century, the Hebrews saw their God as an impersonal force, so great, so holy, and so far-removed from man that his name could not even be spoken.*

Above: Playing the drum for the dancing of the shaman in Tunisia. ***Below left:*** The crouched, shuffling/dancing shamanic walk, the drum and rattles, the wig and dark makeup, and the pointed hat, all suggest Herne the shaman. This was particularly the case with the man's behaviour. He advanced on each of the young women in a somewhat threatening sexual manner, then danced on to the next. ***Below right:*** Cuban shamanic figure. This shows a Voodoo-like version of the Dark Helper. The rooster sacrifice in the shaman's hand is symbolic of fire and fertility, and the mask and headgear are phallic symbols.

The shamans sang, danced, and jumped over fires in sexually symbolic fertility rites, some involving the besom, the broom-like phallic rod.

We can see this Herne/Pan depicted in ancient neolithic cave paintings as well as in medieval illustrations where he is holding the besom, and right on into the twentieth century where, as Santa Claus, he still clutches a rudimentary broom. He is Merlin the Magician of King Arthur's legends; Shakespeare mentions him in *Merry Wives of Windsor* and *A Midsummer Night's Dream;* his witches appear in *Macbeth;* and, to this day, he still appears in numerous rituals in isolated islands and backcountry areas.

On a recent visit to North Africa, I recognized Herne in a folkloric show in Tunisia, complete with shamanic dance, dark face, phallic ornaments, and, as always, busy scaring young women (see illustration). I was told that he was a very ancient (pre-Muslim) folkloric character who also scared children, but that no one remembered exactly who or what he was or from where he originated. Even in Cuba I found an early nineteenth-century painting showing a shamanic Voodoo figure with ritual objects.

Herne/Pan's shamans led the Winter Solstice rituals, initiated the new year, rewarded the good, punished the bad, officiated at the sacrifices, and headed the fertility rites. These people had existed peacefully for thousands of years until, as European archeology shows, they began to erect defenses and palisades. Burned villages, remnants of bronze and iron swords, and other signs of warfare testify to the violent invasion by Celtic and Germanic tribes—the new conquering, warrior aristocracies.

When these Celts, Germans, Greeks, and Romans first came into contact with the Olde Religion, they already had their own panoply of gods. As was their custom, they simply added Herne/Pan to the list, reducing him to the role of a mischievous, sexually-obsessed, sometimes ridiculous, minor god or slave. We come across him constantly, bearing a variety of names from a variety of times and regions: Pan, Faun, Sylvanus, Priapus, Satyr,

Bacchus, and the mysterious, horned Celtic god, Cernunnos. In Britain he was not only remembered as Herne, but also as Puck, a name related to the Anglo-Saxon word *Bogey,* still used in "Bogey-man" for a scary, devilish figure. In Wales, the name was *Boucca.* All of these names were related to *Bog,* the Slavic name for God.

Many of the fertility rites and customs of the Olde Religion continued even after the Germanic god Wodan was introduced by these early conquerors. Wodan/Odin also had much in common with Christ; he had for days been hung on Yggdrasil, the shamanic Tree of Life and Wisdom, with two ravens, one on each side of him; there he suffered from thirst, was stabbed by a spear, and somehow resurrected (compare to Jesus on the cross, the two criminals at his side, his thirst, and the spear wound). Wodan was not only a warrior god, but also the bringer of sunshine and gifts. In return, sacrificial harvest gifts had to be left for his holy steed, Sleipnir. Like today, the gifts were left in socks, boots, and clogs.

When, after 400 years of Roman military occupation, Christianity became the state religion of Rome, the Romans had little trouble forcing the Gaulish tribesmen, who lived south and west of the Rhine, into giving up their Celtic-Germanic religion for Christianity. The Church found the Olde Religion of the poor to be a far tougher nut to crack. The Church was incapable of understanding the idea of an omniscient nature spirit which was (like nature itself) both creative and destructive at the same time. Such thinking was alien to the Church. To them, Christianity represented the battle of good versus evil. In their theology, good and creation were synonymous with God, while evil and destruction stood outside, against God, led by Lucifer, a dissident angel also known as Satan, the adversary. The Church now taught that Herne was the same as Satan; the shamanic witch and Duyvel were also labeled Satanic.

Thus, the mischievous, but basically benevolent, old Herne/Pan, who for 10,000 years had represented the spirit of the hunt (openly sexual and adorned with horns and animal skins), was now used by the Church to represent the visual image of Satan. By giving this Devil distinctly evil and frequently Semitic features, the Church managed to deal two strikes with one blow and (particularly in Spain) encourage anti-Semitism.

At the time, the Roman Christian Church held absolute power, including the right to burn heretics alive. As a result, the Olde Religion and its celebrations soon became hidden. Herne/Pan, however, was not that easily defeated. Christianity had originally moved into Western Europe as a political religion, the religion of the ruling class of the oppressors. The poor, and particularly the forest-dwellers, felt much closer to Herne/Pan, the spirit of their ancestors. For centuries, Herne's worship (the cult of nature, life, love, and death) continued quietly until the Protestant Reformation broke the power of the Inquisition and the Roman Church. Many adherents of the Olde Religion came out of hiding and enjoyed a revival of sorts, until the Protestants and Puritans forced them back underground, with witch trials and the suppression of the joyous, if somewhat licentious, celebrations such as Maypole dancing and Xmas. In England, under Cromwell, the laws against witches stayed on the books until 1736. The last execution there of witches took place in 1716, when a mother and her nine-year-old daughter were hanged. In England alone, a total of 30,000 people were legally executed as witches.

Because of its many obvious connections with the solstice celebrations and the Olde Religion, the celebration of Christmas was forbidden by the English Puritans, who called it both Papist and pagan, and in America replaced it with a non-controversial Thanksgiving harvest feast. It was all in vain; there, too, the common people refused to let go of Herne/Pan and their beloved 10,000-year-old celebrations.

In the sixteenth century, the Low Countries (now Holland and Belgium), through royal marriages and inheritances, became the possession of the King of Spain and were treated as colonies. In 1581, in a precedent-setting Declaration of Independence (later used as a model by the Americans for their own), the Dutch northern provinces disowned their Spanish king after having revolted against his Spanish occupation forces, as well as against the Roman Catholic Church and the Inquisition, and joined the cause of the Protestant Reformation.

This revolutionary war lasted for eighty bloody years, during which time the Inquisition and cruel (often Moorish) Spanish occupation forces committed horrible atrocities against the Dutch population. It seems that at this time, the Dutch changed Zwarte Piet—their version of Herne/Pan (Saint Nicholas' dark slave; or the devil, according to the Church). If the Church insisted Piet was the devil, then he should be made to look like one; a Spanish one—one of the hated Moorish-Spanish Inquisition soldiers, notorious for their cruelty. It was a fine bit of anti-Spanish propaganda. If children did not behave, this Spanish devil would drag them back to Spain in his sack, to hand them over to the Inquisition, the real hell. (Similarly, during World War II, the Dutch might have dressed this devil up as an SS storm trooper threatening to send the kiddies to a concentration camp.)

How strong the pagan beliefs were, and how tenaciously they stuck to their traditions in spite of persecution, can be seen in a recent BBC documentary about the Spanish-owned Balearic Islands. The population of these nearly-inaccessible islands never liked the mainland Spaniards and their Inquisition and continue to resist the Church to this day.

Herne, the Horned One, is alive and well here. During the winter holidays they have a wild, joyous celebration with fires, led by a sensuous, masked, horned figure, who—although not quite sporting an erect penis—appears with a fire-spouting piece of firework held in his crotch in a distinctly lewd manner. With this fiery appendage, he then attempts to scare the young women. It is amazing to see this obviously popular, joyous ritual of fire and procreation celebrated in about the same manner as it probably was thousands of years ago.

It is, by the way, also a perfect illustration of the bringer of Light, Sex, and Fire—the Lightning Serpent, Loki, and the fallen

Above: The androgynous shaman, from a very old Frisian cookie mold. The Herne/Pan shaman spoke for both polarities of the world around him: creation and destruction, male and female, Yin and Yang. He, consequently, appeared in female attire at times. Note the horns in the headdress, the solar emblems on the sleeves, the Tree of Life on the upper skirt, the female sexual symbols (hearts and roses), and the besom (broom), which for centuries remained his symbol of sexuality. *Below:* This detail, showing the two small animals at the shaman's feet, may represent two holy Nordic horses, which can still be found on American Pennsylvania Dutch barn doors.

archangel Lucifer,[9] who were all punished by God for giving these gifts to man. Why the Church objected to this gift, and to the joys of sex, is a bit of a mystery.

The seventeenth- and eighteenth-century opposition of the Christian Churches to Xmas and Saint Nicholas was reflected in the controversies which surrounded the Dutch *speculaas poppen* (called *leb* cakes in German, from the Latin *libitum,* meaning "offering"). These cakes replaced various animal and human sacrifices which, at one time, had been dedicated to pagan gods. First the Catholic Church and, later, the Protestant Church fumed and passed multiple ordinances forbidding the making, selling, and eating of these popular holiday cakes. To no avail; they are still sold today. The bakers simply changed the names and designs slightly, dressing old gods and shamans as seventeenth-century ladies and gentlemen, while leaving tell-tale symbolic clues in their designs.

Since these cakes were baked in carved wooden molds, some of which still exist, we can study the designs today. Unfortunately, hardly any exist from before the fifteenth century, wood being a perishable material, and since the Church ordered the burning of the more obviously pagan ones. I did, however, come across one from about 1480, which shows a Herne/Pan-type figure with solar emblems, holding the besom/broom, dressed in women's clothes, and wearing what looks like a mummer's mask or head-dress with horns. At its feet are the holy Germanic horses (see illustration).

Thanks to the persistence of folklore, traces of Herne/Pan worship and of the Olde Religion still exist today in Santa Claus, and Sinterklaas and his Dark Helper, as well as in many other Xmas traditions. I can only conclude that the original ancestor of our modern Santa Claus is none other than the mythological Dark Helper—a faint memory of Herne/Pan, the ancient shamanic nature spirit of the Olde Religion.

9. *Lucifer: in Latin,* luci *(light) and* fer *(iron), thus "the bringer of light and iron."*

Seven

Saint Nicholas and the Dutch

Some Americans remember that their Santa Claus was named after the Dutch Sinterklaas (a contraction of Saint Nikolaas), the winter holiday figure of the Dutch, who was brought to New Amsterdam (now known as New York) by seventeenth-century settlers. Two centuries later, with the Dutch long gone, Bavarian-born American artist Thomas Nast was assigned to draw this Santa Claus, but having no idea what he looked like, drew him as the fur-clad, small, troll-like figure he had known in Bavaria when he was a child. This figure was quite unlike the tall Dutch Sinterklaas, who was traditionally depicted as a Catholic bishop. Who he drew was Saint Nicholas' dark helper, Swarthy, or Black[1] Pete (a slang name for the devil in medieval Dutch), the shamanic Herne/Pan (known in Europe by many names).

In newly-Christianized areas where the pagan Celtic and Germanic cults remained strong, legends of the god Wodan were blended with those of various Christian saints; Saint Nicholas was one of these. There were Christian areas where Saint Nicholas ruled alone; in other locations, he was assisted by the pagan Dark Helper (the slave he had inherited from the Germanic god Wodan). In other remote areas, where the Church held little power, ancient pockets of the Olde Religion controlled traditions. Here the Dark Helper ruled alone, sometimes in a most confusing manner, using the cover-name of Saint Nicholas or "Klaus," without in any way changing his threatening, Herne/Pan, fur-clad appearance. (This was the figure later used by the artist Nast as the model for the early American Santa Claus.)

The Catholic Saint Nicholas also had a confusing past. He was a compilation of two separate saints (one from Myra in Asia Minor, the other from Pinora), both of whom were—as the Church nowadays admits—nothing more than Christianized water deities (possibly related to the Greco-Roman god Poseidon/Neptune).[2]

This now-apocryphal Saint Nicholas was venerated, not only as the patron of children, but also of sailors, merchants, thieves, and prostitutes (the latter four obviously considered as being in somewhat the same category). He was supposed to have performed charitable deeds (such as the giving of a dowry to two impoverished young maidens) and miracles (the resurrection of two infants who had been slaughtered and pickled by an evil butcher). After the Vikings

---

1. *The terms "black" and "white," as used in this book, do not refer to race or color, but are used in their medieval sense of dark as evil and light as goodness.*

2. *In the 1970s, Vatican Council II formally stated that no Roman Catholic bishop(s) by the name of Nicholas had ever existed, and that the legends attributed to this saint had no Christian origin and probably came from pagan traditions.*

raided the Mediterranean, they brought the Christian Saint Nicholas cult from Italy to Northern Europe, and there proceeded to build Saint Nicholas churches for the protection of their sailors. When, for instance, William the Conqueror's fleet was hit by a storm during his invasion of England, he is known to have called out for protection to Saint Nicholas. Although in those days, church services only mentioned Saint Nicholas as the protector of seafarers, they initially condoned a blending of the Mediterranean Nicholas myths with some that had been attached to the pagan Germanic god Wodan and to those of the even earlier Herne/Pan traditions.

By absorbing such pagan feasts and traditions, the Christian Church could subtly bring in its own theology: in this case, establishing the good Saint Nicholas, bringer of love and gifts, while grudgingly allowing the presence of the Olde Religion's Herne/Pan, but only as a slave to Saint Nicholas. Thus, in parts of Europe, the Church turned Herne into Saint Nicholas' captive, chained Dark Helper; none other than Satan, the Dark One, symbolic of all evil. His only remaining tasks now were to carry the bag, scare maidens and children into devout behavior, and drag sinners and pagans off to the Christian hell. Yet in spite of this character assassination, the poor masses continued to see in this enslaved Dark Helper a reflection of their own enslavement. He remained their Herne, thumbing his nose at the Christian Church; a mischievous, nostalgic reminder of the days of their own free and lusty pagan past.

In Holland and several other European countries, the Saint Nicholas figure is still highly esteemed. He appears as a tall, dignified, bearded, white-haired old man, dressed as a Catholic bishop, complete with cloak, mytre, and pastoral staff, a seemingly genuine Catholic saint, but with a bizarre, quite unsaintly habit of riding through the skies on a white horse, followed by his Dark Helper. It seems that our Catholic saint inherited some of these customs from the pagan Germanic god Wodan, who had also been a bearded, white-haired old man, also dressed in a hat and cloak, carried a staff (or spear), rode a holy white horse, and dragged along the same dark slave/helper on a chain.

Black Pete, the "grandfather" of our modern Santa Claus. Known in Holland as Zwarte Piet, this eighteenth-century German version, is—like his ancient shamanic ancestor—still horned, fur-clad, scary, and less than kind to children. Although portrayed as the slave helper of Saint Nicholas, the two are, in many villages, blended into one character. This figure often has the name Nikolaas or Klaus, but has the swarthy appearance of the Dark Helper. He is known by a variety of names throughout Europe: Grampus, ru Klas ("rough Klas"), Hans Trapp, Klawes, Ashenklas, Klas Bur, Bullerklas, Joseph, Pelzmarte, or sometimes in female form as Berchte, Budelfrau, Befana, or Buzeberght. The date when the figure appears also varies.

Above: The author's father, dressed and made up as the traditional Dutch Saint Nicholas. *Below:* The Dutch Saint Nicholas (Sinterklaas) and his Dark Helper (Zwarte Piet). In Holland, Belgium, and parts of Germany, the old Saint Nicholas cult has remained more or less unchanged to this day.

The Dutch Sinterklaas brings gifts to good children, while bad children are harassed by Zwarte Piet, the Dark Helper, who—brandishing his peculiar broom-like rod—threatens to put sassy young women and naughty children in the sack in which he has carried the gifts, the idea being that he will take them away to some terrible place in Spain (where Saint Nicholas, for no known historical reason, was supposed to have come from). This, of course, never happens since the good Christian Sinterklaas always intervenes on behalf of the naughty child—provided the child promises to better his or her ways. The bad (pagan) Dark Helper is then admonished by Sinterklaas and ordered to stop threatening the children.[3]

Next, Sinterklaas distributes gifts to all "who have been good" (or until the twentieth century, to all "who knew their prayers"). In exchange, the children are supposed to leave food offerings for the saint's horse (usually hay and carrots), placed in either a shoe or stocking. In some areas, a glass of gin is also left as an offering for the good saint himself, but I rather suspect this to be an apocryphal, modern custom to keep up the "spirits" of our modern shamans. When, by daybreak, the offerings have disappeared and been replaced by gifts, it proves that Sinterklaas has indeed paid a visit during the night.

We can clearly recognize in all this the lesson taught the pagans by the Christian Church, here represented by Saint Nicholas: You may enjoy your old fall/winter feasts, as long as you have learned your prayers and become good Christians. You will then be rewarded, but if you have not done so, you will be dragged away to hell by your own fearful, pagan past and its representative, the dark Herne/Pan—who is none other than Satan himself—unless you repent, here and now!

---

3. *This bit of theatre used to be highly effective in keeping the kiddies in line, but modern child psychologists seem to disapprove of such treatment. As a result, the part of the Dark Helper is now frequently played by ladies of dubious youth wearing tights and black-face, acting like some friendly clown and handing out gifts to children, whether they behave or not. So much for modern child-rearing!*

These samples of Dutch Christmas wrapping paper from the 1960s show many of the symbols and aspects of the Saint Nicholas and Zwarte Piet legends.

Like Santa, Sinterklaas and the Dark Helper were also supposed to have the peculiar habit of entering homes through the chimney—a rather undignified, messy access point.[4] Although this was admittedly possible through the great medieval fireplaces, it has become a bit harder to achieve with today's central heating.

Nowadays, the Dutch Saint Nicholas does not always come as a thief in the night. Following a (quite recent) Dutch tradition, he arrives by steamboat "from Spain" with his white horse and Dark Helper, who is now assisted by a dozen or so other associate Dark Helpers, is then received by the mayor of the city and given a big parade through town, after which he personally visits certain lucky families.

The use of the Dark Helpers has recently led to ridiculous accusations of racial prejudice, with pressure to use "white" helpers. This is a silly situation since Herne was never negroid, but only the Church's presentation of a swarthy, satanic force of darkness. Poor Herne; he's had a rough time over the years.

In other European countries, the details, names, and dates of celebration may differ, but the characters and rituals tend to be similar.

In the Czech republic, Saint Nikolas is lowered from heaven on a golden string.

In Denmark, the Santa Claus figure (called "Yul Man") is a recent revival. The truly traditional characters are the Nisser, mischievous, gnome-like characters with red stocking caps, who in the old days used to be quite scary—part of a whole clan of furry, devilish creatures. In Sweden, a similar elf-like "Tomten" rides the old pagan god Donar's goat.

In Sarajevo in Bosnia, Saint Nickolas appears with gifts for the children in spite of the war and shelling. He is assisted by a small black devil who scares the children.

---

4. *In the early Middle Ages, the chimney was thought to be the way through which spirits entered and left the abode.*

In parts of Italy—in spite of all its creches with the Christ Child—there also remains a scary, old, witch-like creature (with a broom) named Befana, who—like the Dutch Sinterklaas and his helper—enters the house through the chimney, takes the food offerings, and leaves presents. This female, witch-like version of the Dark Helper also exists in parts of Austria and Germany, and is known there as Budelfrau, Berchtel, or Buzebergt, suggesting that, like shamans, Dark Helpers could be either male or female, or cross-dressers.

In Britain, where Cromwell so violently eradicated the Olde Religion, Saint Nicholas was mostly forgotten, until he was imported from America as Santa Claus in the second half of the nineteenth century. But as we know from Charles Dickens' *A Christmas Carol* with its Spirit of Christmas Present, vague old traditions remained. This character seems to be blended from Greek customs involving their god Dionysus (or Bacchus, to the Romans) and a pagan, god-like figure, part Druidic high priest, part Herne the Hunter, usually shown dressed in long, green, fur-trimmed robes (see illustration on following page). Since, like the American Santa Claus, he was a vestige of Herne/Pan (not the Christian Saint Nicholas), he carried the broom-like rod. In Cornwall, this same figure still had horns, as did so many of the continental Dark Helpers. Parts of the British backcountry also remember the pagan Herne the Hunter, Horned King of the Forest, who, together with his holy oak, is mentioned by Shakespeare in *The Merry Wives of Windsor* (act IV, scene IV). That he is far from forgotten today was proven by his recent appearance in a British television series about Robin Hood, the implacable foe of the Germanic Normans and defender of the oppressed poor forest villagers. In the story, he is selected to become Herne, the shamanic spirit of the forest.

In Germany, Saint Nicholas' Dark Helper is a swarthy, horned, frightening little man, always brandishing the besom. He is known by many names: Knecht Ruprecht (servant Ruprecht), or in Bavaria, Pelz Nickel, meaning "fur-clad Nick." In Tyrol, the picture is even clearer; there the Dark Helper is Klaubau, a scarier version of the British Herne the Hunter, a chained, furry, black-

103

*Saint
Nicholas
and the
Dutch*

Among the middle class in Britain, a genteel form of the Dionysian winter revelry was remembered and blended with memories of Herne's nature spirit, as seen in this nineteenth-century illustration of the Ghost of Christmas Present from Dickens' *A Christmas Carol*.

faced, horned creature. In other districts, he is called Hans Trapp, Klawes, Klas Buer, Klapperback, Pelzmaerte, Saint Peter, Ashenklas, Bartle, or Grampus.

In certain German children's games (an excellent source of ancient traditions), the Saint Nicholas figure itself is the Dark Helper, a devil who wants to punish the children, but is stopped from doing so by Christ. This Saint Nicholas/devil is obviously not a Christian saint. This reminds us of the bizarre fact that the names Old Nick,[5] Old Nick Bogey (Bog or Bogey was a pagan and Celtic god), Saint Nick, Olde Saint Nicholas, or Nick, were all—at least as far back as the sixteenth century and probably long before that—synonymous with the pagan devil (shaman); suggesting that, here too, the Christian aspect of Saint Nick was only skin-deep.[6]

In other places in Europe, the customs connected with the Dutch and German Saint Nicholas are attributed to Saint Peter, and elsewhere to Saint Marten, and are celebrated on those saints' birthdays. This was probably inevitable because of the confusion in the early Middle Ages when Church authorities brought out their new calendars and insisted on anchoring centuries-old folk festivals to specific new saints' dates. Since local slaughter/harvest feasts varied with latitude and climatic conditions, the same feasts ended up on different saints' days (see Chapter 3).

As you can see, many of these old customs resemble those associated with the modern Santa Claus, but what are their origins? Where exactly did they come from before Saint Nicholas, or even before Wodan? The answer is that the earliest ancestor of Santa Claus existed thousands of years before this phony fifth-century saint was supposed to have been born.

---

5. *Nick was an early folk name for the devil, such as in the word "nickname," meaning not a Christian name, but a pagan first name, a name given by Nick, the devil.*

6. *The names Nick, Klaas, and Klas come from* nikker *(Old Dutch) or* nicor *(Middle English), meaning "goblin" or "waterspirit." This may explain why the Catholic saint created to replace a pagan water deity was given the name Nicholas and protected those who traveled over water.*

The modern, international Santa Claus. In 1931, the Coca-Cola Company, intent on expanding its market to children, decided to use Santa Claus as its advertising vehicle. Haddon Sundblom was assigned to design a new large and jolly Santa dressed in red and white, the Coca-Cola Company colors.

This Santa by the Coca-Cola Company appeared in 1936.

In 1941, this Madison Avenue Santa marched off to World War II, alongside Coca-Cola, and conquered the world.

The last "Coca-Cola Santa" appeared in 1964.

The Family Tree of Santa Claus

Established Religious Institutions

Nature Religions Folk Tales/ Peasant Traditions

Greek Era

The Greek religion began around 2000 B.C.E. with the Indo-European pantheon, which included Pan (now a minor sex, forest, and nature spirit). Their main god, Zeus, had a son, Apollo, who was a resurrecting sun god.

Mithras, solar god

Roma Catho

Roman Era

The Roman religion, which developed around 800 B.C.E., contained a mixture of the old nature religion and the Indo-European pantheon. The Roman religion soon absorbed the Greek gods, such as Zeus, who blended with the Roman god Jupiter. Herne/Pan was remembered by many names, but only as a minor sexual, forest spirit. The Roman priesthood later became the Catholic priesthood (the pope is still called Pontifex Maximus).

Early Middle Ag

Saint Nicholas
In the early Middle Ages, the Catholic Saint Nicholas was s posed to take the place of the gods whose feasts had been c ed on his saint's day. In actua customs of the pagan Herne/I the Nordic/Germanic god Wo blended with those of the sai Holland, Herne/Pan, formerly Wodan's slave Eckhart, conti exist as Saint Nicholas' helpe Zwarte Piet.

Pan

Zeus

Apollo

Indo-European Culture

The Indo-European religion existed about 8000-4500 B.C.E. and probably grew out of the shamanic hunt and nature spirit cult. It then developed a pantheon of anthropomorphic gods, including a stern main god with a son, the solar god, who was friendly to mankind.

The old shamanic Herne figure became Pan, a sexual nature spirit. In Western Europe, four distinct, overlapping cultures emerged from this foundation: Celtic, Germanic/Nordic, Greek/Roman, and the Iranian solar god culture.

Germanic/Nordic Culture

Wodan/Odin
The Germanic/Nordic belief structure entered the scene around 800 B.C.E. The chief god was Wodan, who led a pantheon of anthropomorphic gods, somewhat similar to the Greek and Roman pantheons. One of the members of the Germanic/Nordic

pantheon was Wodan's slave Eckha (Herne/Pan, the shaman or nature spirit), the "captured" deity of conquered people. The Germanic/ Nordic tribes worshiped trees, but also knew the concept of a resurrecting solar god.

The Horned Shaman

The shaman as Herne, the Horned Spirit of the Great Hunt, dates back to at least 10,000 B.C.E. This was part of an animist philosophy in which the Spirit of Nature was impersonated by shamans. It continued to exist in Europe as the pagan Olde Religion, which survived until the beginning of the seventeenth century. It still exists within some cultures.

Herne

Celtic Culture

The Celtic culture began around 1000-750 B.C.E. Little is known about their early religion. They had a horned god, Cernunnos, who resembled Herne. Their

later gods were a mixture Germanic/Nordic gods. Th were a powerful, mysteriou later absorbed by the Cath

Cernunnos

Horned Shaman

10,000 B.C.E. 8000 B.C.E. 4500 B.C.E. 2000 B.C.E. 1000 B.C.E. 800 B.C.E. 0 C.E. 200 C.E. 400 C.E. 600 C.E.

The return of the Xmas tree. Since the eighth century, the Christian Church tried to stop the pagan veneration of trees and fire, but never quite succeeded. With the Protestant Reformation, many of the ancient pagan customs resurfaced, as seen in this painting (1521), the earliest known German painting of an Xmas tree. The figure on horseback is not the pope or a Christian priest. The headdress has only two crowns and no cross on top, and the mantle is decorated with green leaves, telling us that he is a nature god, shaman, or priest-king of a pagan religion.

Giftwrap from the 1960s showing St. Nicholas and Black Pete handing out holiday gifts.

Dutch folk art, a collage hanging of Saint Nicholas and Zwarte Piet, his slave (the Dark Helper/Herne/Pan figure). Note the ever-present symbolic broom/rod. The dark demeanor of the helper was—in the eighteenth and nineteenth centuries—confused with his being negroid, which he was not. The medieval Christian Church had portrayed him as "dark," meaning evil or satanic; later people thought it cute to present him as a rascally little black slave, which today has led to accusations of racism.

The monotheistic Roman Christian religion emerged as a blend of religions used to unite the faltering Roman Empire, and still exists today. It is centered around the teachings of Jesus Christ, who—like the Persian Mithras and other Indo-European resurrecting sun gods—was the son of the one and only god. It absorbed the Mediterranean cult of the Mother goddess in the form of Mary, the mother of Jesus, and was backed by a "pantheon" of saints, many of whom were but thinly veiled former pagan gods. One of these was Saint Nicholas.

St. Nicholas

Saint Nicholas Cult

Renaissance

Gothic Era

Late Middle Ages

es

p-
pagan
lebrat-
ty, the
an and
lan
t. In

ued to

The Modern World

The French Revolution and the nineteenth century reduced the power of the churches and saw a return to many pagan customs, including Saint Nicholas, Zwarte Piet, and the Xmas tree. This is the early development of Santa Claus in the United States.

Black Pete

The Protestant Reformation

The sixteenth-century Protestant Reformation broke the power of the Catholic Church. For a while, there was a resurgence of Herne/Pan and the Olde Religion with a return to pagan customs (including the Xmas tree), until the Puritans and Calvinists forced them underground once more.

Sinte Klaas

Sinte Klaas/Santa Claus
The American Santa Claus first developed from a vague memory of the Sinte Klaas of the Dutch settlers of New Amsterdam, poeticized by Clement C. Moore. This figure was a blend of the Catholic Saint Nicholas, the Germanic/Northern god Wodan, and old Dutch settlers.

Robin
Goodfellow

Zwarte Piet

Thomas Nast (1840-1907)
The Bavarian shamanic figure Knecht Ruprecht was used as the model for the American Santa Claus illustrations by Bavarian-born artist Thomas Nast. In some parts of Europe, this figure was Saint Nicholas' Dark Helper. Saint Nicholas' name was used by this pagan figure, or the Dark Helper still operated on his own as the the ancient pagan Herne/Pan shaman.

The modern, international (commercial) Santa Claus is known in different cultures as Father Christmas, Pere Noel, Father Winter, Kerstmanetje, etc. This figure originated in the United States, then spread world-wide in 1932 as part of the Coca Cola Company's (and other commercial) advertising.

All these names were given to the Herne/Pan shaman:			
* Bartel	* Frau Gaude	* Klapperbock	* Pietje Pek
* Black-Man	* Frau Harke	* Klaubauf	* Robin
* Black Pete	Grampus	* Knecht Ruprecht	* Robin Goodfellow
Budelfrau	* Heks	Mother Berchta	Robin Hood
Buzebercht	* Herne	* Nickel	Silvester
* Cerne	* Hobb	* Niklo	Sunderoom
* Cernunnos	* Holda	* Olde Horne	* Witch
* Dark Helper	* Kaije	* Old Nick	* Warlock
* Devil	* Klaai	* Pelzmaerte	Zwarte Piet
* Duyvel	Klaasoom	Perchta	

(* denotes labeled as Satan by the Catholic Church)

Santa Claus

f Roman and
Celtic Druids
religious order
lic Church.

"For Santa

Eight

Ancient Roots

To rediscover our roots and expose the origins of the Santa Claus figure requires historical, cultural, and religious research into a grey past of which there are no written records. Consequently, much depends on studies of parallel primitive societies which still exist (or existed in the recent past), and on the study of European culture and anthropology, which, surprisingly, only began in earnest after World War II.

The Santa myth turns out to be one of the oldest and most tenacious myths of Western society, in spite of the fact that, as we know, the Christian—as well as the earlier Germanic—religions did all they could to take over and/or destroy the popular myth of Santa's ancestors. Three areas of research are important.

Races and Cultures

Two thousand years ago, Western Europe was inhabited by many different races, tribes, and cultures: among them were the early primitives, the Celts, the Germans, and the Roman-Latins. These races and cultures followed upon each other, but also co-existed and mixed. The early primitive culture with its prehistoric origins, for instance, co-existed with later cultures up to the seventeenth century, and traces of it still exist in many places.

Religions

Among the races and cultures, there existed two radically different religious groupings:

1. Religions viewing nature as a living entity: Primitive/shamanic and Earth/Mother-matriarchy concepts.

2. Religions with male anthropomorphic[1] gods: Celtic/Germanic, Roman/Greek, and Christian (Roman Catholic and, later, Protestant).

Like the different races, these religions arrived one after the other, or in some places, next to and in conflict with one another. It is important to realize that all of Western Europe's anthropomorphic religions (including Christianity) were, or ended up as, male, warrior religions, forced upon the common people by conquerors and the ruling classes set up by those conquerors.

Traditionally, religion has always been an efficient means for oppressors to control the hearts and minds of populations; this happens to this day in many countries. Out of a need for self-preservation, most common people pretended to submit to the new

---

1. *Anthropomorphic: "in the image of man."*

religions, while they quietly continued to follow their own cultural traditions and religious beliefs. As in all situations of this kind, some of the people tried to curry favor with the occupation forces by betraying friends (as at the time of the Inquisition). Others joined religious orders to try, with a moderate degree of success, to work from within the system to accentuate the spiritual, cultural, and humane aspects of the new religion; often blending in the best of the Olde Religion with the new. Consequently, remnants of the conquered religions have continued to exist in the Christian era—even until today. The Santa Claus myth is one of them.

Occupations

The gathering of wild herbs and seeds and the hunting of small animals by both men and women was typical of the early primitive pagans. This, at first, created a society and philosophy which was not property-oriented (and, consequently, peaceful), in which men and women were equally respected. The invention of agriculture by the women, combined with the mystery of childbirth, strengthened women's positions at times and occasionally led to matriarchies. This was later followed by the keeping of cattle, which created the concept of property (and, consequently, greed, theft, and war).

The hunting of larger animals and herds could only be carried out by organizing joint hunts between clans, on what had always been communal hunting grounds. When the clans gathered at specific lunar or solar dates, each clan identified itself with the hides, masks, and other symbols of their clan's totem animal. When the hunt was over, the clans celebrated for several days with a communal sharing of the kill, followed by ritual dancing, fertility rites (sex), as well as plain old carousing, contests, bragging, and storytelling. In later days, when the days of the great hunts were over, these traditions continued at fall/winter harvest and slaughter feasts.

Stone-age people were not as primitive or handicapped as some of us might think. Six-thousand-year-old Norwegian rock carvings show skiers (as today, on both long and short skis). Tests by archaeologists have proven that a couple of men could cut down, burn, and clear an acre of pine forest in less than four days, using only the stone axes of the period.

When men went beyond hunting to the domestication and grazing of cattle and to agriculture, it introduced a new—and often resented and disputed—concept of property rights, particularly with regard to the newly-domesticated animals. Up until then, all animals had always been "fair game" for anyone, a situation which, as in the old American West, led to tribal conflicts and warfare, bringing about a warrior cult and an aristocracy of the strongest, with a new, paternal, warrior religion. This situation became typical of the pagan Celtic, Germanic, and Roman tribes, with their constant intertribal battles and cattle raids. The later Christian aristocracy continued along this same path, even claiming ownership "for the King" of all big game, fish, and lumber.

The early Christian Church first established itself in Western Europe in the territories south and west of the Rhine—an area which had been under the firm military and cultural control of the Romans for more than 400 years. Now, backed by what remained of the military power of Rome, the new Christian Church launched major, and at times violent, efforts to eradicate all vestiges of surviving pagan worship, particularly of the tenacious, ancient Olde Religion, as well as of the more recent Celtic and Germanic religions.

When, 500 years later, Christian missionaries tried to convert the various warlike, independent tribes who had never been dominated by Rome, or who resided in distant islands and border areas (such as Lithuania, the Alps, the Dutch marshes, and Welsh and Scottish Highlands), they had to act in a more cautious and diplomatic manner. As a result, the Church tended to allow popular pagan feasts and customs to continue, provided they were now linked to the saints' days of the new Christian calendar.

The winter culling of the herds (a slaughter common in the days when there was no way to keep enough fodder to see all the animals through winter) followed the final harvest. Culling obviously occurred at different times, depending upon the climate in which the harvest was gathered. In western Europe, this was between November 3 (the day of Saint Hubert, the horned patron saint of the hunt) and the time of the shortest day (the Winter Solstice). In Holland, this event was celebrated on the day of Saint Nicholas (December 6).

On the eve of December 6, the myth told that this bearded, white-haired old "saint," clad in a wide mantel, rode through the skies on a white horse, together with his slave, the swarthy Dark Helper. This reluctant helper had to dispense gifts to good people, but much preferred to threaten them with his broom-like scourge, and, at a sign of his master, would gleefully drag sinners away to a place of eternal suffering.

Those familiar with European mythology will recognize three separate entities:

Wodan/Odin: The Germanic/Nordic sun god[2]; man's friend, the mysterious Schimmel rider (see below). Dragging his dark and devilish slave Eckhart along on a chain, he rides through the stormy skies. He leads the Wild Hunt, eluding, and finally subjugating, the powers of evil. He also wears a broad-brimmed hat, a wide mantel, holds his spear, and rides through the skies (replace his hat with a bishop's mytre and the spear with a crozier, and we have the Dutch Saint Nicholas).

The Schimmel: Name for a holy, shining, ghostly, dapple-grey or white horse. Wodan's holy steed, Sleipnir; the sacrificial white horse

---

2. *Some disagree about this, since the Romans saw Wodan as identical to their god Mercurius. Baldur, one of Wodan's sons, is also thought to have been the sun god. Both theories may be correct, since the image of Wodan seems to have been different at different times.*

of ancient Germanic worship, known in England as Old Hob, whose image can still be seen on European and Pennsylvanian barn doors. In prehistoric days, the horse was sacrificed and its flesh eaten, after which the entire dried hide and skull were used to adorn the gable of the farm, to bring luck and protection.[3] Up to the twentieth century, a horse's skull, with clacking jaw, was used in village rituals in England and Wales, as well as on the Continent. The Christian Church was so opposed to these pagan horse sacrifices that they forbade the eating of horse flesh, which is the reason why many, to this day, consider eating horsemeat "taboo."

The Dark Helper: Eckhart, the slave of Wodan, is Herne/Pan, the early pagan Horned One, Herne the Hunter, King of the Forest, the Dark One; the ancient, prehistoric, fickle, shaman/nature spirit of the hunt, song, dance, music, and sex. He remained very popular, as late as the days of Shakespeare. This being could be male or female, or both in one; he sometimes dressed in women's clothing, and often carried the broom/besom, the ancient symbol of fertility with which he used to threaten young women, and later children.

Behind the false front of the Christian Saint Nicholas, we have here a continuation of the pagan myth of the Nordic god Wodan, riding through the skies in the wild hunt, on the holy Germanic Schimmel, with Eckhart, his Dark Helper-slave; the latter being none other than the Herne/Pan shaman of the defeated, primitive forest races.

This is a typical example of the blending of pagan and Christian religious and mythological thinking under the early Germanic conquerors, later adapted by the Roman Catholic Church in the early Middle Ages. To these pagan myths were added ancient Mediterranean legends of Nicholas the Christian saint. Now, centuries later, this mythological blend still underlies the American (and now international) Santa Claus legend.

---

3. *The use of the horseshoe for the identical purpose is a later variation of this superstition.*

The European Santa Claus, also called "Father Xmas." Father Xmas came out of hiding in the early nineteenth century after the Church had lost much of its power as a result of the French Revolution. He wore a loose, hooded fur (or green fur-trimmed) robe, and carried a horn, Xmas greens, or a tree, as well as Herne's notorious besom rod and sometimes a fiery torch. Note the Jack-the-Joker at his waist, a phallic symbol.

Bringing in Olde Christmas. A very rare, mid-nineteenth-century illustration of an Xmas party in England with Herne/Pan. The use of the words "Olde Christmas" indicate that this is not the usual Christmas, but an archaic custom. We see the figure of the dancing, bearded (masked?), horned (or perhaps wearing candles on his head like Lucia), Herne. He stands in a bower of evergreens with lots of mistletoe overhead. Above him, a figure appears to be riding a broom; another rides a Yule log. He holds another standard emblem of the shaman, the trident (later made into a Satanic symbol by the Church).

This early nineteenth-century Christmas illustration is full of ancient symbolism. On a throne with hearts, and flanked by a dejected cupid, a somewhat bemused, horned Herne/Pan figure looks down at three well-to-do Christian ladies who dole out charity to the grovelling underpriviledged. Herne, in an unsubtle sexual gesture, "stirs his lady's cup" (slang for sex) with his phallic Tyrsus-like rod. This rod is surrounded by little nude figures in poses of abandon emitting from his lady's "spoon" (slang for sexual play), and by fluttering faeries, doing what looks like a witches' row dance with a tiny horned Herne figure (upper right corner). Two prankster jesters drink and look on dejectedly. In typical Victorian fashion, the illustrator tut-tuts and pretends to disapprove of the sexual, pagan Xmas festivities by showing disapproving, nun-like shadowy figures in the background.

At one time, researchers concluded that Saint Nicholas was nothing more than a memory of the pagan god Wodan made to fit the Christian faith. But what about his mysterious Dark Helper (a.k.a. Herne the Hunter, Lord of the Forest, Eckhart, Pan, Puck, Robin Goodfellow, Nick, Pelz-Nickel, Zarte Piet, Knecht Ruprecht, the witch Befana, to use just a few of the many names by which this figure was remembered)?

No, there was more to it than that, for it is the much older Herne/Pan, the Dark Helper, the slave of Wodan and Saint Nicholas—not the Celtic/Germanic god Wodan—who is the ancestor of our modern Santa Claus myth. To find out why, we must look at the relatively recent anthropological theories about early Europe.

When
Santa
Was a
Shaman

Nine

Traditions

Holland is an excellent country in which to study ancient European traditions. Here, as in other Germanic countries and in Britain, many animal sacrifices, rituals, and traditions of the Germanic and Olde Religion have persisted for centuries, and have ended up as part of the Xmas and Saint Nicholas celebrations. In the sixth century, the enlightened Pope Gregorius the Great wrote to the English Bishop Augustinius:

> *Do not destroy their pagan temples, but make them into Christian churches named after*

saints. Out of custom the people will continue coming and will venerate their new God. Their animal sacrifices should be maintained, but changed; instead of being sacrifices, they will supply a Christian meal in the honor of God.

The Nordic (and Roman) sacrificial animals had been the ox, the sheep, and the swine. As they were led off to slaughter, they were decked with garlands of flowers and leaves. In modern Dutch homes you may see Delft, ceramic figures, or cream pitchers in the shapes of those sacrificial animals, adorned with painted wreaths of flowers as was customary 2000 years ago in pagan rituals. In certain villages, the ancient custom exists unchanged; there the live animal is adorned with wreaths of flowers and, after circling the church three times, is ceremoniously paraded to the butcher where it is ritually killed for the celebration meal.

In time, it became too costly and inconvenient, for many families, to slaughter and sacrifice such large animals. They replaced them with bread offerings baked in the animal's shape, or with animal cookies, such as those carved in the old Dutch *speculaas* cookie molds, the so-called *koekplanken* (cookie planks). These traditional cookies are still popular winter holiday snacks.

One of the sacrificial animals was the boar, the wild pig, dedicated to the Germanic thunder god Thor (another giver of lightning). Until the beginning of the twentieth century, a boar's head with an apple in its mouth was ceremoniously served at grand Xmas dinners "bedecked with garlands of bay and rosemary," as sung in the Oxford Boar's Head carol. This dish is still served at the festival of the same name at Oxford University in England.

The large German marzipan Xmas piggies, as well as the "piggy bank" of our youth, with its painted garlands of flowers, its fattening-up with pennies, its moral teachings of saving and generosity, and its final ritual "slaughter" by breaking it around Xmas time—they too are remnants of this ancient sacrifice.

Above: The sacrificial ox. Here seen on a late-eighteenth-century print, the ancient pagan sacrifice of the bull or ox—traditionally decorated with garlands of flowers—still exists after thousands of years. *Below:* Boar's head formally presented, once the holy sacrifice to the Germanic god Thor.

Above: The Santa shaman on a rare eighteenth-century *speculaas* cookie mold. His headdress suggests horns and he dances to the music of the curved bow, while the leaves on his sleeves identify him as the Wild Man, another name for the shaman of the Olde Religion (the penis could not be shown, of course). *Inset:* This ancient dancing shaman is the ancestor of the one above.

One can only guess at the origins of other winter holiday customs which still exist in some countries. What, for instance, was the origin of the custom of giving nice gifts (called "surprises," or—in Scandinavia—Yulklap) hidden in multiple wrappings, or inside seemingly undesirable objects (like a hollowed-out potato) and accompanied by a derisive, or even insulting, poem in metric rhyme? We know that this custom also existed 2000 years ago in Rome, and probably long before that. Was it part of the "Lord of Misrule" winter holiday customs, which allowed slaves, servants, and students to temporarily reverse their social position, permitting them to insult, or "lord it over," their masters? But why the valuable gift inside the common, or even repulsive, container?

It is amazing how long the memory of even bizarre and horrible rituals, such as human sacrifice, can persist. It is said that certain clans of Nordic pagans launched their Dragon-ships over the bodies of young female sacrificial victims, tied to the front of the vessel so as to be crushed upon launching. With the coming of Christianity, this gruesome offering was replaced by a sacrifice of animal blood and later, wine (nowadays champagne). Until the late nineteenth century, however, carved figureheads of the upper torsos of bare-breasted young women still adorned many a ship's bow, more or less in the same place where the poor creatures had been crushed to death in pagan ceremonies 2000 years earlier. A coincidence? I doubt it.

When I was a child in the 1920s, it was still customary, during the winter holidays, to call in the servants and give them each a huge *speculaas* cookie called a *vrijer* (lover). It bore the image of a seventeenth-century gentleman or lady, but upon closer examination, one could see a solar emblem on the man's coat and a small dog (symbolic of faith) at his feet. This, at one time, had been the image of the Nordic god Wodan, the bringer of the sun.[1] The maids received the "male" cookie; the male servant, the "female."

---

1. *In Nordic mythology, Wodan won a fight with the ice god and led his people south to the sun, an obvious reference to an Ice Age leader who led his people to warmer lands.*

The female figure represented Freya, the goddess of love and sex (the Nordic equivalent of Venus), who always had a bird on her shoulder. The idea behind all this was that this gift would bring the servants luck in finding a mate and getting married.

Originally, such gifts had been fertility symbols. Marriage without children was considered disastrous for a family and, because of that, Nordic farm maidens did not get married until they became pregnant. As a matter of fact, Frisian farms, until the end of the nineteenth century, had a back room in which the eligible daughter slept. Here she was visited by her lover(s), who had to climb in through the window. Once pregnant, she would decide which of her lovers she wanted to recognize as the father, after which they were married.

Fertility rites were connected with the fire rituals of the Summer and Winter Solstices and with the slaughter celebrations; some involved big bonfires over which the young men and women would jump. Others involved more sensuous games; in its day, the holy Druidic mistletoe probably sanctified a bit more than just an exchange of kisses.

Some of the sacrifices came from the Germanic culture, such as the golden pagan rooster (dedicated to Donar, the god of thunder) which still protects the top of the steeple of many a European village church, supposedly offering protection against fire and lightning. This shows how long superstitious congregations felt more comfortable clinging to the trappings of their pagan beliefs than to those of Christianity. The Church tried rather lamely to switch the meaning of this pagan rooster to the rooster who crowed thrice at the denial of Jesus by Peter.

Another ancient sacrificial animal was that Olde Religion symbol of evil and witchcraft, the black cat. The Church was always particularly anxious to stop these ancient pagan sacrifices, which they associated with Satan. One of these had been that of the "Duyvel's Kater" (Devil's Tom-cat), the black cat, long a symbol of bad luck, which only Herne and his witches could control. Anyone familiar

Above: The battle between the cat and the rooster symbolizes the conflict between "evil" paganism (the cat) and "good" Christianity (the rooster, herald of the resurrection, who also crowed thrice at Peter's denial of Christ). The trouble is that the rooster itself was a pagan symbol and sacrifical animal, as was the cat. The pagan rooster, symbolizing fire and sexuality, conveniently became Christian in the Middle Ages. *Below left:* Cats flying with witches. The dog was the male's hunting companion, but the cat was the pagan woman's (and witch's) companion, protecting the grain crop and food supply from rats and mice. It its effort to blacken the witches of the Olde Religion, the medieval Christian Church authorities portrayed the cat (a sacred pagan sacrificial animal) as a creation of Satan, a "familiar," lewdly cuddled in the witch's lap, who also accompanied her on perverse (sexual), broom-straddling, aerial escapades. As a result, thousands of cats were burned alive, along with their mistresses. *Below right:* To primitive man, cats—big or small—were symbolic of evil and sudden death. Even domestic cats can be incredibly ferocious fighters. Why cats became holy animals is not completely clear.

with truly wild cats knows what vicious fighters they are when cornered, and it must have been an amazing sight to see the first tame cat quietly purring away on some witch's lap.

The black cat is still subject to superstition, but when the Christian Church forbade the people to perform their cat sacrifices (done at Halloween?), the villagers secretly replaced the ritual with the sacrifice of a loaf of bread baked in the shape of a cat. Over the centuries the name was contracted to *duivekater* and its meaning was forgotten. After World War I, bakers no longer baked it in a cat shape. When I was a child, only a few bakers in Holland knew how to bake this delicious, dark brown, decoratively-carved loaf, now no longer in cat shape, but more like a large fish without a head, though with a tail on each end. You can see a similar loaf in Jan Steen's painting *De Bakker Oostwaard,* at the Rijksmuseum in Amsterdam. The bakers vaguely remembered that there had been something special about this bread and they only baked it for the winter feasts and Easter. Now it is baked in a round shape and no one remembers the cat, or the original meaning, at all.

In Europe, many traditional recipes are still in use, though with time, sugar has replaced honey as a sweetening agent, and the Eastern spice trade has made the Dutch *speculaas* far tastier and spicier than the similar German *lebkuchen,* which uses the more ancient ingredients. By the same token, the ancient custom of giving a person a piece of pastry or bread baked in the shape of his ancient Nordic rune initial—the reason for which seems to be now totally forgotten—still exists, but, in the Netherlands, is often replaced by giving people a piece of chocolate in the shape of their initial.

On Saint Nicholas' Day, choir boys used to pick a "boy-bishop," a kind of king for a day with whom they were allowed to run the church for that day, while also being permitted to go begging for handouts. This may have been a vestige of the Olde Religion's election of a substitute king (god) for a day, in which a lucky man was treated with great respect and was given full royal power. But for only one day—after this he was put to death as a sacrifice. Less lethal traces of this custom still exist in France, where on Twelfth Night (the twelfth night after Christmas) a large cake is divided among the guests. The one who finds the hidden gold coin (nowadays a bean) is king for that day (without getting sacrificed the next day).

When the Dutch revolution and the Reformation overthrew the Spanish king and his Catholic Church, the bishop aspects of Santa were considered objectionable by the now-Protestant government. The Church had never had a strong grip on the Nordic countries, and long-suppressed Pagan customs resurfaced to such an extent that the Puritan, Calvinist Protestants made an effort to get rid of Sinterklaas and Xmas altogether, calling these celebrations both Papist and pagan. The 10,000-year-old spirit of Herne/Pan and Sinterklaas was, however, far too deeply-rooted and popular. It has outlived the Celtic/Germanic cults, the Inquisition, and the Puritans.

On the Dutch Wadden islands, the Sunderums (from "Sunder Klaas" and "Klaas-Oom"; Uncle Klaas) still go about—as they did thousands of years ago—in their primitive pagan costumes made of heather, dune grass, shells, and chicken feathers, trying to scare everyone. Others blow centuries-old ten-foot (three-meter) long *buffelhoorns*, through which they also talk in a scary voice. Some of the younger, more aggressive men, called *baan-vegers*, or "trail-sweepers" (brandishing Herne/Pan's broom), scare the girls, but also dance with them (in more primitive days, they reputedly ventured out to raid cattle and rape the girls of other villages). Women and children are chased back into their houses and "beaten" if they disobey. This probably is meant to protect them from the herd of frightful ghosts who are said to appear and threaten the world at the time of the disappearance of the sun, at the Winter Solstice.

In other remote areas of Europe, men also dress as devilish figures or in scary masks (similar to the English mummers, vestiges of the old clan leaders in their animal clan masks and furs). People light huge fires; there's the ringing of bells, blowing of horns, and swinging of rattles to bring back the sun and to scare away the evil powers of darkness which are accused of trying to eat up the sun. We continue to perform some of these rituals at New Year's Eve parties, where, until recently, costumes and masks were traditional. The use of noisemakers, car horns, and general ruckus are a must when ringing in the New Year. The difference is that today's people perform such rituals without any idea as to why they do so.

If some of these customs seem strangely primitive to you, you're absolutely right: they are. The customs of our North European ancestors of 2000 years ago—a mere forty generations ago—were indeed barbaric and primitive. These ancestors lived at the edges, or in clearings, of the world's largest forest; a dark and ancient jungle that stretched from the Scottish Highlands across Britain, across Europe, through Russia and Siberia, all the way to the other side of the world, on the Siberian coast and the Pacific Ocean. No one was known to have ever crossed the entire forest.

This was the true realm of Herne the Hunter: the great forest without mercy, a forest which had been there as long as man could remember. It was a forbidding place of immense 1000-year-old oaks and of gigantic wild cattle; the so-called auer-ox, the last of which was killed in Germany in the sixteenth century. (These wild bulls were much larger and more aggressive than modern cattle, and their horns were wider than those of Texas Longhorns, who, along with the Spanish fighting bulls, are supposed to be their descendants.) The forest also harboured other terrifying animals, such as the gigantic cave bear—an animal larger than any bear alive today—as well as regular bears, buffalo, huge deer, and packs of large, aggressive wolves. On the other hand, this forest was also a haven for free men and women, where they could hide from conquering foreign oppressors and conversion.

To members of my generation, the memory of this great forest is still very real. Most of the stories read to me as a child reflected a deep fear of the ancient forest: Little Red Riding Hood, Tom

Thumb, Robin Hood, Jack and the Beanstalk, Hansel and Gretel, Sleeping Beauty, and not to forget, Snow White, who was saved from death in the forest by seven of Herne/Pan's Little People. Judging from the present popularity of the werewolf, Dracula, and other forest-based horror movies, even today's youth still seem under the spell of the ancient, subconscious, Jungian fears of the dark, ancestral Hyrcean forest.

The reader may think that all this only relates to prehistoric times or grey antiquity, but in some areas, the fear of the forest was very real as recently as a couple of generations ago. Take the story my maternal grandfather told me. He was raised on a farm in the Belgian Ardennes (a small remnant of the Olde Forest), and as a small child, he had a long walk back from school each day through the forest. As he walked home on this particular snowy, winter day, he was surprised to see his father and several other farmers on horseback galloping up to him, their rifles at the ready. It seems that a pack of wolves had been seen trailing him through the forest!

Ten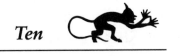

The Great Hunt

Toward the end of the last ice age, many clans were in the habit of meeting one or more times a year, when the great herds migrated, in order to join together in the Great Hunt. This forerunner of our Xmas and Saint Nicholas feasts was a sacred event, a hunt in which even rivaling or warring clans might join forces to enable them to corner and hunt large numbers of fast animals of large size, such as wild horses, to slaughter them and smoke their meat for the oncoming winter. It normally was hard for the men of a small hunter-gatherer clan to hunt and kill such

129

fast and wary animals; they just did not have enough individuals in the clan to chase and corral[1] them.

In our modern world of maps, clocks, and calendars, we don't realize what a difficult task it then was to establish a given date and meeting place for clans coming from, say, a hundred miles away. It was the task of the shamans to establish the next meeting place and date each time. This depended on past experience and on newly-gained information about the migrating routes of the animals.

It must also be remembered that most people at the time probably only had names for three numbers: one, two, and three. Roman numerals remind us of that: II and III are obviously two and three fingers, while V is the whole hand (four fingers and a thumb, forming the "V" between the fingers and the thumb). Consequently, four is named as five (the hand) minus one finger: IV; and six as VI (the hand plus one finger). Ten is two hands above each other (X), eleven is the fingers of two hands plus one (XI), and so on.

Terms like east, south, west, and north were unknown but were probably roughly described as "where the sun rises," "where the sun is at its highest," "where the sun sets," and "across from where the sun is at its highest." Months were counted from one full moon to another (which, of course, does not quite match the yearly solar cycle), and years would have been counted as so many "winters." The year itself was divided, as it still is, by natural phenomena: spring (the greening), summer (when the sun is high), fall (when the leaves fall), and winter (when the sun disappears).

Rather than give a dry summation of such events, I will try to give a (fictional) account told in the bardic tradition by an old shaman, of what he, as a boy, experienced at his first Great Hunt, somewhere on a plain in Europe. How he, on the days following this slaughter, butchering, and meat curing, participated in the great,

---

1. *The word "corral" is from the Latin* currere, *meaning "to run"—in other words, to chase on foot.*

raucous eating feast and took part in the dances and rituals where he, for the first time, met a large number of strangers who were not direct relatives or of his own clan.

The Great Hunt

I am Bjorn; I have been this clan's shaman for many winters. Our clan's totem animal is the bear. I am old, having seen as many winters as four times the fingers of my hands, or so they say. Soon I will die like most other men and women of my age—since my teeth are gone and I can no longer eat meat or roots—when the fruit and berries I live on will be out of season.

As an orphaned boy, originally born in the Clan of the Fox, I was given the name of Bjorn (bear) after surviving a mauling by a cave bear. I only survived because I remembered what my aunt once told me: "If, while searching for berries, you ever trespass on a bear's grounds and a bear takes hold of you, don't scream or yell or fight to get loose; just talk quietly in his ear and apologize for trespassing. Tell him you're sorry and that you won't take his berries anymore, and that the berries taste better than you do, so please let you go."

I did, and so did the bear; he let me go, but only after gouging a solid piece of flesh out of my back.

I only survived because of the wisdom of my aunt, who was a witch[2] as well as being our shaman, and who knew how to heal a festering wound with spiderwebs and powdered fungus. Actually, my full name then was "He whom the bear let go of," and I have stuck to my promise to that bear and have since never eaten any of his berries, at least not when he was around.

---

2. *Before the coming of other religions, "witch" was an honorable title meaning a wise one who could predict things (such as the solstices) or achieve things "miraculously" (such as making fire). The terms "shaman" and "witch" are often used interchangeably. The most important shaman/witch was known as "Duyvel."*

But I am digressing; I was going to tell you about my very first Great Hunt.

I had then just passed my rites of manhood in a painful and strenuous ritual. As I told you, our shaman was my mother's older sister; an ugly, but kind and very wise, old woman, who was training me as her assistant. She knew every herb and berry in the forest and taught me which ones could cure a fever, and how to make fire (which, being secret magic, I may not tell you about).

On this day, she took me to a flat-topped hill on which stood a tall, dead tree from which all the branches had been removed. This place was taboo and no one but our shaman and her assistant could approach it without danger. Nearby lay several white stones. She pointed her stick at one of the stones and told me that when the shadow of the tree first touched this stone, the clan would travel for four days in the direction of a distant mountain which I could barely see. Here, on a plain at the foot of this mountain, several other clans, also guided by their shamans, would show up on about the same day.

This was to be the first time in many winters that our clan would again participate, since there had been bad blood between the old man of our tribe and the old man of another clan, all because of some woman he had stolen after a previous Great Hunt. I was very excited because, even though our clan was large—as many as the fingers on the hands of two men and one more—here there would be one hand plus two fingers just of clans, which is more people than anyone can count!

I had only once seen a person from another clan, the Otter clan. A boy had lost his way, wandered far, and then had fallen and broken a leg. He told me this, but his speech was quite different from ours and I had trouble understanding him. He died soon thereafter and I covered him with stones, as I had seen our people do—so the wolves would not disturb his spirit before it could find a tree to live in. I kept an odd string with several large, translucent beads which he had worn. See, I am still wearing them.

Our voyage to the gathering ground was uneventful. Although it was warm in the sunshine, one could, in the shadows, already feel the chill of the oncoming winter. The tops of the distant mountain ranges showed a light dusting of snow and few leaves remained on the trees; the tall grass was yellow and dry. Thousands of migrating birds were flying past, all heading toward the sun. Although we saw no migrating herds as yet, there was an abundance of other game, but mindful of my past experience, I gave a wide berth to a couple of large bears who were busying themselves catching fish in a fast-running stream. As we neared the gathering grounds, I smelled the many campfires well before I saw their smoke rising in the still, cool air.

We were met by the shaman of the Otter clan, who greeted my aunt (our shaman) with some ceremony, until he noticed me and started jabbering away excitedly and so rapidly in his strange dialect that I could no longer understand him. It turned out that the beads I was wearing were a particular token of the Otter clan. Only after my aunt told him the story of the lost Otter boy who had died did he calm down and, patting me on the shoulder, even allowed me to keep the beads, which he said were of something called amber.

We learned from him that the migrating horses had not as yet appeared, but were expected the next day. Scouts from the Horse clan were observing their progress from the hilltops and would send up a smoke signal to warn us of their approach. When the sun was at its highest, there was to be a meeting of the clans to discuss the hunting strategy and to perform the horse-hunt dancing ritual. Until then, I had some time to wander around by myself.

We were on a plain; a plateau which sloped down gently toward the side of the rising sun. Both on the side of the setting sun and of the midday sun, there was a sheer cliff dropping down as deep as the height of several men. Across from this, on the other side of the plateau, the steep slopes of the mountain were cut by a pass through which we expected the migrating horses to emerge the next day. The campsites were a fair way off on the downward slope, so as not to alert the horses to our presence too soon.

I walked down to the campsites where our clan's shelters had already been set up, with our clan's emblem, the Fox mask, hanging on a post. From a distance, I could see the various other clan masks hanging on the shamans' shelters at the other sites: the Wolf clan, the Badger, the Horse, the Serpent, the Deer, and nearby, next to the creek, the Otter clan. Our people were busy gathering firewood and building smoking-racks inside a shallow cave in the mountainside. Here we intended to butcher, smoke, cure, and dry the horse meat we hoped to obtain tomorrow.

I sat down near the creek and ate some of the roots and hazelnuts I had gathered earlier in the day. I watched in fascination as some of the girls of the Otter clan stood waist-deep in the creek washing their garments, then hanging them on branches to dry in the sun. At this moment, the girls wore nothing but their clan's amber bead necklaces. Like my aunt, even the young women of my clan tended to be short and heavy, with very wide hips and buttocks, large, pendulous breasts, and dark, matted hair. These Otter girls, however, were tall and slender, with small, firm breasts and hair of a light reddish hue. I was particularly fascinated by two of the girls who looked identical; so much so that I could not tell them apart. I had never before seen twins.

One of them stared at me, then walked up and asked me why I wore the Otter beads. I had to repeat the story of the lost Otter boy who had died and given me his beads. She said he was her cousin and had been missing. Her name was Ute and her sister's name was Dag. I wanted to get to know them better, but just then the clans were called away for the planning of the hunt and I had to join our shaman.

All the clans were gathered around with their shamans in a smaller circle in the middle. The shaman of the Horse clan spoke, or rather chanted, the words to a dancelike ritual, in which he and two other shamans acted out the part of the horses, while several hunters danced in simulation of the hunt. The scouts had seen the first horses in the mountain pass and the herd was expected at dawn the next morning. All campfires were to be extinguished, so that no smell of fire would discourage them from coming out on the plain.

As soon as the horses would emerge onto the plateau, the Horse clan scouts were to move in at their rear and block off the pass by setting fire to the dry grass. Meanwhile, the assembled clans would form a line across the slope of the plateau and, with the prevailing wind at their rear, also set fire to the grass; thus cornering the animals between the mountains, the fire, and the cliff. The most skilled hunters from each clan then were to move in for the kill, using their spears, while older men would stand near the bottom of the cliff to dispatch any animals that fell or jumped down trying to escape the hunters and flames. The women and children would form the line on the slope and set the fires, while the older boys—like myself—had to try to spear or chase back any horses trying to break through the line of fire. Should, however, any pregnant mares or mares with colts try to escape, we were to let them go, for these mares would help create the herds for future Great Hunts.

All these instructions had been accompanied by a beating of drums and chanted responses from the audience. The session ended with a kind of "ooohhming" ritual and a dance and plea to the spirits of the horses, asking them to forgive us for what we were about to do and thanking them for helping to nourish us through the coming winter months; for the horse was a sacred animal and there was a taboo on killing it at any other time of the year.

As soon as the crowd dispersed, I hastened to our campsite to cut myself several light spears with my old flint knife and, not having flint spear points, I went to harden the points at the Deer clan, where a very small fire was maintained to light the firebrands needed to set tomorrow's grass fires. I noticed a tall Deer boy carving a peculiar piece of wood, which he called an atlatl: a spear-thrower. His name was Hoge. His clan had learned to make this simple tool which allowed a hunter to throw his spear with far greater force and accuracy. He showed me how it was used, and I decided to make myself one sometime soon.

I joined some of our women to look for food, but except for a few dried-out berries, we found nothing, the grounds having been thoroughly picked over by those who had arrived here before us. I filled myself with water from the creek and fantasized about gorging myself on fresh-roasted meat after tomorrow's hunt.

The night was clear, with a full moon. Without campfires and being very hungry, the crisp cold penetrated my bones, in spite of the two old wolf hides I had wrapped myself in. I dreamed of a ghostly herd galloping through the skies, led by a snow-white stallion, which then somehow changed into Ute, the Otter girl, running nude through the stream, laughing, with her wild red hair flowing in the wind.

We were awakened by the look-out who had seen the smoke signal from the scouts: the horses were in the pass! Moving silently, we grabbed our weapons. The women had made their fire brands and stood ready to light them at the Deer clan fire. I grabbed my spears and quietly climbed to the place where the foot of the mountain reached the sloping plain. Not only did it offer me a good hiding place from where I would be able to see the horses emerge from the pass, but I had noticed that here the soil was rocky, with only sparse grass, and that the fire would not burn well here. It was a place through which the herd might try to break through.

None of our people could be seen, and except for a couple of noisy ravens, there was total silence.

Suddenly, I saw him: a solitary scout, a dapple grey stallion, standing there silently, listening, sniffing the air and pawing the ground. He seemed larger and more delicately built than any horse I had seen before. After a moment, he galloped around the plateau to the edge of the cliff, then toward the slope. He stood there, like a grayish-white ghost in the light morning mist, sniffing the air some more and pricking his ears. After some hesitation, he turned and galloped back, disappearing into the pass.

The sun had risen and started to heat the air, and a mild wind was blowing from the valley. What was taking so long? Had the stallion become aware of our presence and alerted the herd? I heard a rumbling and the stallion reappeared at a gallop, followed by a cluster of mares—some with colts—then by the rest of the herd. It was a magnificent sight, seeing these beautiful animals enjoying the warm sunshine, and galloping around the field. They turned toward the slope on my left. As if out of nowhere, a line of hunters appeared from behind the tall grass, screaming and yelling as they moved forward. The stallion stopped in his tracks, whinnied loudly, and swung around at full gallop, followed by the herd, seemingly back to the pass, only to be met there by hunters with burning torches, setting fire to the grass at the canyon entrance.

The air was full of the cries of the clans, the whinnying of the terrified horses, and the crackling sounds of the fire. I had in the past gone on hunts with my uncles, but there I had always been taught to move silently—only using hand signals.

I had never heard so many voices, such noise, as I did now. The wind had picked up somewhat, fanning the flames, causing them to roar up the hill, pushing the crazed horses into an ever-shrinking area. Through the smoke, I could see several of them going over the edge. Some of our hunters were darting between the flames, getting close to the horses, stabbing them with their spears.

Then it happened. I saw how the Ghost-Stallion tried to round up his mares, whinnying loudly, rearing up and trampling a hunter who tried to block his way. Followed by the remaining herd, he charged straight at the hunters who scattered before him, then galloped full speed through the flames, toward the bare patch in front of me. Several of the horses hesitated before the flames and were killed, but many of the mares and colts followed him through the thin line of fire to the safety of the burned-out ground in front of me. I stood transfixed as he passed me within three feet, looking right at me with his large black eyes, nostrils flaring. Then he was gone in a cloud of dust, smoke, and ashes, followed by the remains of his herd thundering down the slope, causing our women to run out of the way like so many rabbits. A last mare limped toward me, singed and blinded by the flames, crippled by a broken spear sticking out of her abdomen. Taking careful aim, I sank my spear into her heart, killing her instantly, hoping someone would do the same for me if I ever ended up like that.

The Great Hunt was over and many horses had been killed, as many as the fingers of four men. I was now a hunter, having made my first kill—although it was nothing to be too proud of. There followed the bloody, gory business of butchering all these animals, saving the hides and cutting much of the meat in thin strips for drying and smoking, a back-breaking job in which every man, woman, and child had to participate. The clans were now assured of an ample supply of food for the coming winter, as well as for tonight's Great Feast.

The bones[3] of the slaughtered horses were gathered and stacked in two large heaps, to which we added dry branches and logs. The smaller stack was at the foot of a solitary pine tree; the bigger stack was a short distance from there. Tonight would begin the Great Feast, the feast of thanks and celebration of the gift of fire, light, and life, a feasting on mounds of roasted meat, followed by ritual fire and fertility dances, and other initiations.

It is hard for modern man to realize the degree of isolation in which early man lived. Outside of his small clan of some twenty

---

3. *The sacrificial fire made by burning such bones is still remembered in our Xmas and New Year's Eve bonfires (bone-fires).*

to twenty-five closely-related members, he rarely saw any other humans and, when he did, the clan's dialects could vary to such an extent that it could be difficult for them to understand one another. Clans were usually led by a dictatorial old man with full sexual priority and right of first choice or exclusivity over all the females of the clan. This may seem bizarre to the reader, but remember that this was the legal right of the European aristocracy until abolished in 1789 with the French Revolution. It continued to exist informally with slaves and servants well into the twentieth century.

Food could be abundant or very scarce, and, except for meat, most of the common foods and beverages we know today (apples, pears, peaches, oranges, tomatoes, milk, wheat, bread, cheese, sugar, and many others) were unknown. Except for the meat of small animals and occasional carrion, man ate roots such as carrots, greens (like wild celery or dandelion greens), berries, nuts, and the rare, sweet treat, honey. During the winter and droughts he often had to go hungry and spent most of his time scrounging for food.

Thus, for the small hunter-gatherer clans, the Great Hunt was a unique chance to obtain badly-needed extra protein for the winter season, and it was an equally unique opportunity to meet others at the Great Feast that followed.

Eleven

The Great Feast

The feast here described was a prehistoric form of various ancient feasts, such as the Greek Cronia, the Roman Saturnalia, Kalends, and other New Year's Day celebrations, as well as various spring, sowing, hunt, or harvest feasts, including Maypole celebrations, Xmas, Saint Nicholas' Day, and, last but not least, Carnival (a yearly event of unbridled carnal[1] permissiveness).

---

1. *Carnal: from the Latin,* carne, *meaning the pleasures of the flesh, including sexual pleasures.*

Over a period of 10,000 years, the basic elements of this feast—if somewhat modified—continued to exist virtually unchanged, although the dates, as well as the excuses and motivations for its celebration, changed greatly. But let us allow Bjorn, the shaman, to continue his narrative.

When all the butchering was done, we went up to the chosen tree and hung the entrails and certain selected cuts of meat on its branches, adding some of the fat and dry kindling to the stack of bones at its base.[2] We then went to the creek to wash the sticky blood from our bodies, after which I cleaned my garments and hung them on a tree to dry. I lay down in the warm sun, exhausted from hunger and hard work. After a while I woke up, sensing a shadow on my body. Ute and Dag, the Otter girls, were standing over me. Their clothes were drying next to mine, but their lovely bodies were still smeared with the blood of the horses.

"My sister Ute wants you to do the fire dance with us tonight," said Dag, whereupon they both ran off, giggling mischievously, and dove into the creek. I watched them as they washed, but was so tired that I soon fell asleep again.

I awoke to the wonderful smell of roasting meat. Starving and cold as I was, I sat up and saw the red glow of many fires. People from the different clans were milling around, roasting meat, laughing and eating, all mixed together as though they were one huge clan. My clothes were still damp, but I put them on anyway, and grabbing my knife and spear, went over to the carcass of the young mare I had killed that morning. Much of the better cuts of meat had been removed for drying and smoking, but there was plenty left. I cut off a huge side of ribs and meat, sticking them on my spears. Seeing Hoge, I sat down next to him at a fire and positioned my side of ribs

2. *This custom persisted well into the seventeenth century in the rural areas of several pagan Baltic states and with East Siberian natives.*

over the glowing embers. The heat made the steam rise out of my damp clothes, so I took off my top and let the warmth radiate through my body. I was so hungry I could hardly wait for the meat to be done before tearing into it. It was the best food I'd ever eaten; for the first time in my life, I ate enough to really fill me up.

Hoge—who was one winter older than I and had been to a Great Feast before—told me that, when the eating was over, his shaman would have the honor of leading the rituals; this, because the Deer clan is the oldest clan of all and their shaman, consequently, is the Duyvel, the Horned One, the lead shaman in charge of the ritual fire and fertility dances. The Feast is the only time of the year where the old men of the clans have no power over their women and young males; as a matter of fact, these young people are encouraged to get together with those of other clans so that the families will mix their bloodlines and get strong children. They may, however, not stay together after the Feast. The old men then regain full power over their clan and anyone breaking this taboo can cause a conflict between clans, as happened in the past with our Fox clan.

Hoge had just finished telling me all this when I felt a soft hand on my back. "What is this scar on your back?" Ute and Dag had joined us. I proudly told them of my past encounter with the cave bear, as well as the fact that I was our shaman's apprentice, all of which duly impressed them. Near us, several older hunters had been telling each other stories of previous Great Hunts and of hairy encounters with aurochsen, lions, and bears. I felt pretty important when I noticed that even they listened! The girls had a small basket of dried currants and nuts which the four of us shared, along with the remainder of the meat.

We heard the mournful moan of a cow horn being blown, followed by a cacophony of sounds, with much drumming and rattling, all of which was supposed to scare away certain evil spirits of the dead. Brandishing a burning torch, a shaman raced forward and lit the fire at the foot of the chosen tree. Starting slowly at first, the flames soon leapt high up the tree, creating a column of fire, further fed by the dripping fat of the offerings on the branches. The other shamans, wearing the animal masks of their respective clans, performed a wild dance around the tree. Then each lit a torch from that fire, and with much screaming, yelling, and drumming, they ran over to light the big bone fire and some smaller fires. Soon, with sparks flying everywhere, these fires lit up the side of the mountain and I could see their light reflecting, like little stars, in the eyes of the wolves, jackals, and other smaller scavengers who, at a safe distance under the trees, were feasting on remnants of the carcasses of our Great Hunt. It all was an awesome sight.

The shamans, some of whom wore women's clothes, threw large bundles of hemp on one of the smaller fires, then withdrew in a slow, shuffling dance. I recognized the Deer shaman—the Duyvel—standing alone, wearing his large, horned mask, a cow horn hanging around his neck and a burning torch in his hand. As he came closer to the firelight, we noticed that he sported a huge erection (my aunt later told me that this was achieved by rubbing his penis with nettles, a process which, as I later found out, is very effective, but a less than pleasant experience).

The other shamans suddenly reappeared behind us, along with a line of dancing hunters wearing peculiar masks and mantles of grass, seaweed, and rags. They brandished broom-like sticks with which they threatened the girls and young men, ordering us to dance while making lewd gestures and "sweeping" us toward the hemp fire. We knew all this was in fun and part of the ritual, but in the eerie light of the flames, they looked like so many ghosts. I felt Ute clinging to me in fear as they ripped off her clothes and grabbed at her lewdly.

I then heard the voice of my aunt, the shaman, whispering in my ear from behind her wolf mask: "Take her; run and jump over the hemp fires." I did as she told me, dragging Ute along with me, while trying to protect her from the blows and swipes of the hunters. Hoge and Dag followed our example. As we reached the fire, we breathed deeply of the fumes, and with a mighty leap, jumped over the flames, followed by Hoge and Dag. We all landed unhurt, seemingly ritually safe from further harassment. Several others followed our example, but through the flames we could see how other squealing girls and women had been caught by the "sweepers" and were being "raped" by the hunters.

For awhile we sat down to catch our breath until the hemp fumes got too much for us. We giddily withdrew to a more distant fire, where Hoge and I made love to the twins until we all were so tired, we fell asleep.

The distant roar of a lion awakened me. The sun was just rising over the plateau. Ute lay at my side with her arm over my chest; Hoge and Dag also lay close by. Some distance off, where we had butchered the horses, a lioness was guarding a carcass against two hyenas and several vultures. The noise and madness of last night was gone, leaving only the soft hum of insects and chirping birds— peace and silence had returned to the land. Behind me, from where yesterday's bone fires had roared, thin wisps of smoke rose high into the sky. Here and there, groups of individuals still lay wrapped in wolf hides; behind them the blackened skeleton of the Chosen Tree pointed skyward. The Great Hunt and the Great Feast were over. The old men were back in power until the next Feast.

A few days later, Hoge, Ute, Dag and I had to leave with our separate clans, but we agreed to meet at the next Great Feast to carry out a secret plan we had in mind. Before then, we would each stock up on food and flint tools and weapons and would then, at the next Great Feast, elope and form our own clan. One winter later we did just that, which is how the Bear clan was formed by the four of us, plus the two children Ute and Dag had since borne, two dissatisfied young women, and a boy whose father had been killed by wolves. Ute named our son "Little Bear." He became a famous hunter, but was later killed by one of the big people with white hair and metal swords.

Our clan now counts as many members as the fingers of three men. I am the shaman, and Hoge is the old man of the Bear clan. After three winters, we reached a settlement with the other clans and our new Bear clan was accepted and allowed to join the Great Hunts and Feasts.

The basic elements mentioned in this story still form part of our celebrations, not only among Lapps, Native Americans, and Inuit (Eskimos), or in remote European villages and islands, but also in modern Western society. The meetings of the family clans, the festive shared meals (eating and drinking until you're ready to burst), the bringing of gifts to share with friends and strangers, the rituals, games and dances, the bragging and storytelling, the importance of fire, light, and the "burning" tree with its precious offerings, the seasonally tolerated sexual permissiveness (as during Carnival and Xmas and New Year's Eve office parties), the making of loud noises to scare away "evil spirits," the rod/broom, the sweepers, the masks and the mummers, the huge bonfires (with their very name still reminding us of their sacrificial origin)—and on and on.

All these have incredibly ancient roots: they're all with us, these rituals, customs, and taboos of millennia ago, passed on from generation to generation. It would be sad if these ancient cultural roots were completely forgotten, erased from our culture, as they seem in danger of being, by the end of this century.

Twelve

Conclusion

I wrote this book to remind us of the importance of our roots, customs, traditions, and myths, to keep us in touch with our heritage. We should not mindlessly perform yearly rituals without knowing what they used to represent.

There is a certain danger in this, in that it may—to the careless reader—sound as though I encourage a revival of priestly shamanism, primitive religions, witchcraft, etc., complete with sex orgies, ritual rape, bell, book, candle, broom, and cat sacrifices! Nothing is further from my mind; on the contrary, there is a distinct need to have a good look at all this and to debunk the misuse of ritual, magic, and worship.

We live in a modern world and have over the millennia gained much knowledge in matters of science. We have learned to separate science from pseudo-science and no longer have to use the confusing terms of "magic" or "miracle" for events which we do not understand or cannot as yet explain scientifically. We simply try to find out how these phenomena work, using empirical tests and observation. We no longer need ritual chants and dances to teach hunting or sex education, or to cure the sick. We use "magic" computers, books, videotapes, and well-educated teachers, doctors, etc., who, with their modern means, can instantly have the accumulated worldwide knowledge of centuries at their fingertips.

No, why the shaman and the rituals of the burning tree are of importance to us, in spite of all their old mumbo-jumbo, is because primitive man was still close enough to nature to allow him a better sense of his bond with Gaia. Today, only astronomers are aware of the stars. Then, every man and woman slept under the stars and thought and dreamed of them, sensing that the universe was as alive as they were. When they ate meat, it was not something in a plastic package, but something cut from the body of an animal they had had to kill to feed their children. They lived in a symbiotic relationship with the land, the plants, the trees, and all the life forms around them; they were aware of this relationship and, consequently, respected the animals and nature. Death was part of the reality of life.

The rhythms of nature were the personal rhythms of man. He rose with the sun and went to sleep with the evening star. Women were aware of the relationship between their monthly cycles and the lunar cycles, as much as their fisherman husbands were aware of the tidal cycles and the moon.

Modern man has lost much of this personal link with nature and Gaia. Unless he regains it, he will destroy himself and nature around him. He will have misused the gift of fire and knowledge.

Ritual, magic, worship, and celebration are terms and events which must be understood to prevent confusion and misuse. I touched upon them earlier, but I believe a closer look is warranted.

Ritual: A teaching tool used by many higher animals and even by bees. It can be used in a positive way, but is just as often misused to lure participants into a position of subordination to power, authority, and worship, and into accepting magic without proper research. Adolf Hitler and his Nazis used it to gain power over the minds of the population. The notorious Charles Manson used it for its power to control the crime sprees of his murderous "family," while many a "mullah," faithhealer, metaphysicist, and television evangelist has grossly misused it for the purpose of political, financial, or sexual power and gain.

Magic: "The use of supernatural powers to override the laws of nature." Even this Webster definition is nonsensical; if a magic act was proven to achieve such a result, it would immediately lead to a revision of the laws of nature and these "supernatural" powers would then be recognized as actually being natural! The man-made "laws of nature" are certainly not absolute and have (like all laws) undergone frequent and major revisions over the centuries.

Much of what was called "miraculous" or "magical" in the past we know today as science. Our ancestors labeled things as "magical" when a connection with the contemporary laws of nature had not been established, or when these laws needed to be adjusted to match the new discovery. This miracle (after examination of the evidence to eliminate fraud) was then accepted as science and ceased to be magic.

When, long ago, that shaman secretly calculated the length of the sun's shadow to magically predict the exact day of the Winter Solstice and thus was able to "save the sun from being devoured by the powers of darkness," he knew his calculations were "science," but he (mis)used his knowledge to create the false impression that his magical powers extended beyond knowing when the sun would start rising higher in the sky.

He lied and made it seem as though the sun had obeyed his orders and that, consequently, the members of his clan would do well to obey them and his "god" or "channeling spirit" as well. Like all professional magicians, he hid his simple scientific knowledge behind a smokescreen of ritual and hocus-pocus. By doing this, he essentially became a crook, a swindler out after personal power.

Too often such individuals try to impose their own concepts of religion and behavior on others. Instead of saying "According to me," or "My intuition tells me," they say, "God told me" (or even better, "God appeared to me and told me"). They make their own words and thoughts the thoughts of "God." If it then is written down and passed on for a few generations, the religious establishment saves what it believes fits in with its policies. This, then, becomes the canon. It's cast in cement, and don't you dare disagree or ridicule it, or you may get barbecued at the next autodafe,[1] or condemned to death by the Iranian government (such as recently happened to author Salman Rushdie).

To early man, with his limited knowledge of the laws of nature, almost all science was first seen as magic. Even today, a primitive audience may see a personal computer or an instant camera as magical or miraculous. The difference between a scientist and a pseudo-magician, however, is that (hopefully) the first never purposely tries to give his invention a supernatural aura.

Children and immature adults have always looked for shortcuts to satisfy their desires, rather than putting in the time, effort, and creativity needed to do so. Wouldn't it be great to swing a wand or chant a spell and, for instance (using a common male fantasy), cast a spell on that lovely girl you'd like to bed, turning her into your obedient love slave? It would be easier than having to work at winning her love. Or imagine casting a spell and using special numerology to learn the ancient Druidic secrets of wealth and power, to win at Las Vegas. For millennia, unscrupulous individuals—priests,

---

1. *Autodafe: the formal burning of heretics.*

Magi, con-men, and cults—have catered to people's sorrow or selfish desires for such magical, miraculous shortcuts. "I'll worship and offer sacrifices to your god and his power—invested in you as his priest—if you save my child over the thousands of other children who are starving to death." What kind of selfish, evil trading is that? Fortunately, in nature, the essence of fairness is randomness, not preferential treatment in exchange for offerings and worship.

Worship: As opposed to celebration, worship is based on the idea that there is an outside force, a power, which consciously "rules" each of us individually; an entity which sees us as its obedient children or servants. These forces, called God, Allah, Yaweh, etc., demand servitude, based on rules and statements given us long ago, but always via some human, after which it was written down by the same or other "very special" humans, in books such as the Bible, the Koran, and other "holy" works.

Oddly, these gods are always supposed to be in need of pyramidical organizations of human representatives, empowered to speak in their name; representatives who want us to follow their orders and what they insist are this deity's teachings. They presume to talk about worship, love, and charity, but, in actuality, many of them support practices of death, power, and greed, while loving the privilege of chief seats in their gatherings and obsequious salutations in the marketplace.[2]

If we do not worship the deity in the precise manner these representatives order us to, "It" will no longer protect us from "Its" wrath. By pleasing these holy henchmen with the right ritual behaviour and by supplying generous offerings (presumably for the deity), we hope they may, like a king's chamberlain, intercede in our favour and possibly save us from the deity's wrath, either in this vale of tears or in some nebulous hereafter.

Celebration: The exact opposite of worship as defined above. The true shaman celebrated life; not just man's own existence, but that

---

2. *Freely after Luke 11:43 (Jesus and the Pharisees).*

of all nature around him. We are not its servants, but we are part of it (in the same manner that each individual cell of our body, each bacteria in our intestines, is part of our own symbiotic being). We are all interdependent, equal, responsible partners; humans and other creatures, forests, seas, mountains, deserts, and planets. We are all imbued with the spirit of life, and if that is not reason enough for joyous celebration, I don't know what is. We don't have to fear or worship it, because we're an integral part of "It," but, as such, we are also responsible for "It" by our actions.

Consequently, we should stop behaving as infants playing make-believe, expecting some superman, god, king, dictator, political demagogue, guru, or magic formula to rescue us with abra-cadabras, selling us the guaranteed correct guidelines to salvation and great wealth, or any other easy shortcut. It is now up to us personally to think and make decisions, while always questioning so-called authority.

It may seem scary to have to make our decisions alone, instead of having an authority figure telling us what to think or do. It is called growing up, and as soon as we start doing so we will find out how liberating it is, and that we are not alone. On the contrary, we are a symbiotic part of a great, magnificent whole.

We have too long raped and robbed Gaia and are now, within our lifetimes and those of our children, approaching the moment of truth. If we do not want to witness Armageddon and the death of Gaia, it will require major personal sacrifices, which is as it should be, provided these sacrifices apply to all and everyone, not just to the dying masses at the bottom of the pile.

Arrogant Western man has long had a tendency to see himself as more civilized than so-called primitive man—or even Third World citizens—but indoor plumbing, freeways, pollution, and traffic jams hardly qualify us as more civilized.

It pays to remember that 2000 years ago, at the time of Caesar, the Romans also had indoor plumbing, marvelous aqueducts, great international highways and bridges (some of them in use today), and, just as today, they were fighting pollution and traffic jams in the city of Rome. At that same time, some of our Nordic ancestors were still head-hunting, drank *skolls* to their friends' health out of enemy's skulls, sacrificed maidens, and—in some areas—even indulged in cannibalism (in Scotland, the last trial for true cannibalism was held in the late eighteenth century). In spite of that, our Barbarian ancestors thrived and survived, while the presumably civilized Roman Empire ceased to exist.

Like Roman civilization, Western civilization has obviously given us privileges we have appreciated, but it also has a dark side. It has brought us colonial empires, worldwide exploitation by multinational corporations, oil wars, empires, atomic bombs, and generally, non-stop wars (including two World Wars), hunger amidst plenty, explosive overpopulation and the rapid depletion of our natural resources, combined with ozone holes and worldwide, ever-spreading pollution.

Western Christian culture has taught us faith and hope, but alas, like the Olde Religion of Herne/Pan, it also drew us into its dark side: replacing pagan human sacrifice with the Inquisition's public, live burning of "heretics"[3]; and introducing us to the horrors of the Crusades, holy wars, and genocide, all the while condoning slavery and racism.

Are we now to witness the death by commercialism of our oldest myths: those of the shaman and of the Tree of Fire? Have we forgotten the millennia-old teaching rituals, meant to remind us of the dilemma of the gift of fire and knowledge—the gift which set us apart from other animals, allowing us to participate in the reshaping of our planet and its life, but also demanding an unselfish duty of responsibility for its stewardship?

It is the latter point that is so crucial to the future of this world. For centuries, we have acted like small children playing with the

3. *Heretics: literally, "those with other points of view." In this case, the word refers to those who questioned the authority of the Christian Church.*

matches of limited knowledge. We are now becoming young adults who must learn to accept our full responsibility as stewards, rather than abusing that knowledge out of greed. If we continue to procreate irresponsibly like a planetary cancer—or a plague of locusts greedily devouring all the Earth's resources—in a very short while, we will destroy ourselves, along with all of Gaia (our living earth). Nothing will be left but a dessicated, Mars-like reminder of life and beauty that could have been. The choice is ours. It does not have to happen that way.

It has never ceased to amaze me that Herne/Pan existed almost unchanged for some 10,000 years. We first saw him in prehistoric cave drawings in the Dordogne, and when we saw him again in a seventeenth-century illustration, he had not changed one bit. He was still standing, with his musical instrument, in his animal skins, masked and horned; dancing the Dance of Life while aggressively displaying his manhood. He was truly the Spirit of Nature, the raw Spirit of Life letting his light shine brightly in that short interval between birth and death. He survived the next three centuries, but was gradually silenced, sanitized, castrated, dehorned and finally—as his Dance of Life was slowed to a crawl—was presented to us in shopping malls: boozy, old, overweight, grey, and even worse (thanks to Big Business), "cute."

Over the last century, a new god, a god of greed and commercialism, has risen to overrule nature and exploit our planet, a god seemingly determined to cut down all Xmas trees and to enslave Santa even more than Wodan and Saint Nicholas ever enslaved Herne/Pan. This power seems to succeed where Celtic and Germanic gods, the Inquisition, and the Puritans failed. Will life, joy, care, and love enable the tenacious spirit of Herne/Pan to survive, or has Santa Claus been mortally wounded, ending up stuffed and animated in Disneyland?

All this may sound interesting, you may think, but isn't it a bit ridiculous to start worrying about whether or not the myths of Santa Claus and the Xmas tree survive? Really, aren't there more important things to worry about in this world?

Maybe; maybe not. Remember what happened to you as a child, when the "myth" of Santa Claus was so important to you? Santa made you happy, warned you to behave, and scared you a bit, perhaps, but then rewarded your good behavior with gifts. You looked at the Xmas tree[4] in childish wonder and meditated on its flickering candles. It taught you that the beauty of nature and the forest can live in harmony with the flame of the candle, and still give you comfort and joy.

Then, one day, you thought of yourself as quite adult, having found out that Santa was "only" a myth. You were just about ready to toss aside these silly old myths, when you realized that you had to continue the myth yourself, for the sake of your little brothers and sisters—and later for your own children. It was now up to you to carry on the myth ... you had to become Santa Claus.

A myth, like a parable, is just another way to show people the consequences of our human actions. For thousands of years, we have, like little children, greedily exploited the gifts which Earth bestowed upon us, while leaving the responsibility for the survival of the Earth and its other denizens to whatever god we individually followed. We blissfully ignored the fact that it was we who—in exchange for the gift of fire—had now taken upon ourselves the duty of stewardship.

Do we just stand there, bemoaning our loss of innocence, wondering who will tell us what to do next, who will give us the orders? Are we "waiting for Godot"?[5] Someone is not miraculously going to fix things for us. We cannot wait eternally for some parent, politician, or private god to save us.

---

4. There are, of course, many other fire-memory symbols in various cultures, such as the biblical Burning Bush, the Jewish Menorah, eternal flames, or even the energy-inefficient (but oh-so-fascinating and sexy) open hearth.

5. A reference to the famous play of the same name by Samuel Beckett in which two men wait eternally for someone named Godot (God) to come and solve their problems.

The author as Santa Claus.

We tried to make a god in our own image, we tried to run the world as though it belonged to us; we alone made this mess.

It is now up to us, individually and jointly, to initiate the necessary changes, to revitalize the old myth and bring nature and knowledge back into a state of harmony. We must don the mask of the shaman ourselves, and teach the celebration of the Dance of Life—not with magic circles, exotic incantations, and rituals of past millennia that do not relate to today's problems or have been bypassed by science, nor with self-indulgent efforts at exerting our powers over others. Instead, we must live with intelligence, dedication, and self-discipline; by giving up some minor comforts and being less selfish and, above all, with compassion and love for all and everything around us and for the Greater Entity of which we all are a part.

Let us then light the candles on the living tree, while remembering that there is much more to Xmas and Santa than the jingle of a cash register, or a plump actor in a shabby red suit and a cheap cotton beard.

So, here's to Santa Claus and the memory of the Tree of Fire, and a merry Xmas to all of us!

Glossary

Besom/Broom: An ancient symbol of the pagan Olde Religion. Originally a stalk of the broom plant with a tuft of leaves at the end; also an actual broom, sometimes with a short or no handle, symbolizing fertility; the male (rod) inserted into the female (the twigs).

Devil: Also Duyvel. In Christian theology, made synonymous with Satan; the opponent of God. In the pagan Olde Regligion (pre-Christian, pre-Germanic) not connected with evil, but the title of their high priest, the head shaman-medicine man, spokesperson for all forces of nature, both creative and destructive. Lesser shamans (both male and female) were known as witches, meaning skillful or holy; or, according to others, wicka or wise person (from Old Norse).

Legend: A story coming down from the past; especially one regarded as historical, although not verifiable.

Myth: A story, the origin of which is forgotten, which ostensibly relates to historical events, but serves to explain some practice, belief, institution, or natural phenomenon.

Magic: Early efforts at science, accepted without empirical investigation; a part of many pagan religions. Sympathetic magic tries to bring about a desired result by mimicry.

Ritual: Ritual is regarded as of paramount importance in most religions. Sacrifices, mimetic (imitative) dances, processions, plays, games, and feasts are the chief acts of early rituals (see **Magic**).

Taboo/Tabu: Sacred prohibition put upon certain people, things, or acts.

Xmas and Christmas: In this book, I have differentiated between Christmas and Xmas. I use the spelling "Christmas" in referring to the celebration of the mass held in memory of the birth of Christ and his traditional nativity pageants. I use "Xmas" to denote the joyous pagan celebration of the harvest and slaughter feasts; the Winter Solstice and the return of the sun. The X sign, adopted as one of the symbols of the Christian faith, was originally the runic cross of Wodan, which indicated the division of the year into seasons.

Bibliography

Aardweg, B. S. P. V/D. *Sint Nikolaas en Feest en Vierda-gen in Kerk en Volks Gebruiken*. The Netherlands: 1978.

Aho, J. A. *Religious Mythology and the Art of War: Comparative Religious Symbols of Military Vio-lence*. Westport, CT: Greenwood Press, 1981.

Aland, A. *Adaptation in Cultural Evolution*. NY: Colum-bia University Press, 1970.

Allan, T. *Het Eiland Texel en Zijn Bewoners*. Amsterdam: 1856.

Anwyl, E. *Celtic Religion in Pre-Christian Times*. London: 1906.

Aswynn, F. *Leaves of Yggdrasil*. St. Paul, MN: Llewellyn Publications, 1992.

Ausubel, N. *Pictorial History of the Jewish People*. NY: Crown Publishers Inc., 1958.

The (Authorized) King James Version of The Holy Bible. St. Louis, MO: Concordia Publishing House.

Barnett, S. A. *Communication in Animal and Human Societies*. Banton, 1961.

Baumer, F. L. *Religion and the Rise of Scepticism*. NY: Harcourt Brace, 1960.

BBC. "Balearic Islands." From the series *Rough Guide to World's Islands*. 9 December 1992, BBC 2.

Bellah, R. N. "To Kill and Survive or to Die and Become: The Active Life and the Contemplative Life as Ways of Being Adult." *Daedalus*. Spring 1975.

Bibby, G. *Four Thousand Years Ago*. NY: Alfred A. Knopf, 1961.

Bigelow, R. *The Dawn Warriors: Man's Evolution Toward Peace*. Boston, MA: Little Brown, 1969.

Bohannan, P. *Law and Warfare: Studies in the Anthropology of Conflict*. Garden City, NY: Natural History Press, Garden City Press, 1967.

Bowden, C. H. *Short Dictionary of Catholicism*. NY: Philosophical Library, 1958.

Braidwood, R. J. *Prehistoric Men*. 7th ed. Glenview, IL: Scott, Foresman, 1967.

Brentano, R. *Rome Before Avignon*. NY: Basic Books Inc., 1974.

Burian, Z. and J. Wolf. *The Dawn of Man*. London: 1978.

Burland, C. *North American Indian Mythology*. Middlesex, England: Paul Hamlyn, 1965.

Busk, R. H. *The Valleys of Tyrol*. London: 1874.

Bychowski, G. *Oliver Cromwell and the Puritan Revolution*. Zawodny: 1966.

Campbell, J. and B. Moyers. *The Power of the Myth*. NY: Doubleday, 1988.

Campbell, J. *The Hero With a Thousand Faces*. Princeton University Press, 1973.

Campbell, J. *The Mask Of God: Primitive Mythology*. NY: Viking Press, 1969.

Carpenter, E. *Pagan and Christian Creeds; Their Origin and Meaning*. George Allen & Unwin, 1921.

Caesar, Julius. *War Commentaries*. NY: The New American Library Inc., 1960.

Chadwick, H. *The Early Church*. Dorset Press, 1986.

Church, F. P. *Is There a Santa Claus?* Grossett & Dunlap, 1938.

Cirlot, J. E. *A Dictionary of Symbols*. Translated from Spanish. NY: Philosophical Library, Inc., 1962.

Clark, G. and S. Piggott. *Prehistoric Societies*. London: Hutchinson, 1965.

Coon, C. S. *The Hunting People*. Boston, MA: Little, Brown, 1971.

Count, E. W. *4000 Years Of Christmas*. Henry Shuman, 1948.

Crippen, T. C. *Christmas and Christmas Lore*. London: Blackie & Son, 19??.

Cruden, A. *Unabridged Concordance*. Baker Book House, 1953.

Daniel-Ropps, H. *Daily Life in the Times of Jesus*. Hawthorn Books, 1962.

Darlington, C. D. *The Evolution of Man and Society*. NY: Simon & Schuster, 1969.

Davidson, E. *Gods and Myths of the Viking Age*. Bell Publishing Co., 1981.

Dawson, W. F. *Christmas, Its Origins and Associations*. Elliot Stock, 1902.

Dice, L. R. *Man's Nature and Nature's Man*. Westport, CT: Greenwood Press, 1973.

Dickens, A. G., ed. *The Courts of Europe, 1400-1800*. London: 1977.

Dickens, C. *A Christmas Carol*. London: Bradbury & Evans, 1845.

Dickens, C. *The Pickwick Papers*. London: Chapman & Hall, 1838.

The Douay Confraternity Version of The Holy Bible. Los Angeles, CA: C. F. Haron & Co., 1950.

Drew, K. F. *The Barbarian Invasions*. NY: 1970.

Dumond, D. E. "Population Growth and Cultural Change." *Southwestern Journal of Anthropology* (21 April 1965).

Einhard and Notker. *The Stammerer Lives of Charlemagne*. Various translations. (850?)

Eliade, M. *Shamanism*. Princeton University Press, 1964.

Falk, R. *Legal Order in a Violent World*. Princeton University Press, 1968.

Falk, R. *The Potential of Women*. NY: McGraw-Hill, 1963.

Fisher, H. E. *The Sex Contract: The Evolution of Human Behaviour*. London: 1983.

Frazer, J. C. *The Golden Bough*. Avenel Books, Crown Publishers, 1981. (Originally published London, 1890.)

Freuchen, P. *Book of the Eskimos*. Cleveland, OH: World, 1961.

Freud, S. *Totem and Taboo*. London: Routlege and Kegan Paul, 1950.

Fromm, E. *Man for Himself*. NY: Holt, Rinehart and Winston, 1947.

Garcilasco. *The Incas*. Alain Gheerbrant, ed. NY: Avon Books, 1964.

Ginsberg, C. *The Witches Sabbath*. Holland: Wereldbibliotheek, 1993.

Ghesquiere, R. *Van Nicolaas Van Myra Tot Sinterklaas*. Amersfoort: The Netherlands: Acco. No date.

Glacken, C. J. *Man Against Nature: An Outmoded Concept*. Helfrich, 1970.

Glob, P. V. *The Bog People*. London: 1969.

Goffart, W. *Barbarians and Romans*. Princeton University Press, 1980.

Gomme, Sir G. L. *Folk Lore Relic of Early Village Life*. London: 1883.

Graft, Dr. C. C. V/D. *Nederlandsche Volksgebruiken Bij Hoogtijdagen*. Amsterdam: Heemschut Serie, Alert De Lange, 1947.

Grant, F. C. *Ancient Roman Religion*. Liberal Arts Press, 1957.

Grun, B. *The Time Tables of History: A Touchstone Book*. NY: Simon & Schuster, 1982.

Guerber, H. D. *Noorse Mythen; Mythen & Legenden Uit De Middeleeuwen; Mythen van Griekenland en Rome.* The Netherlands: W. J. Thieme & Cie., Zutphen, 1935?.

Haan, Dr. T. J. W. R. *De Folklore Der Lage Landen.* Amsterdam: 1972.

Haining, P. *Superstitions.* UK: Treasure Press, 1990.

Halliday, W. R. *Greek and Roman Folklore.* Harrap, 1927.

Hamer Magazine. Various articles on folk customs. The Netherlands: Arbeiders Pers, midwinter 1941.

Hamlyn, P. *Roman Mythology.* UK: The Hamlyn Publishing Group Ltd., 1969.

Harrison, M. *The Story of Christmas.* London: Odhams Press, 19??.

Hassankhan, R. *Al is Hij zo Zwart Als Roet.* The Netherlands: Warray, 1988.

Hastings, J. *Dictionary of The Bible.* NY: Charles Scribner's Sons, 1937.

Heemskerk, W. F. Van and D. Zinnebeelden. *In Nederland, Uitgevery Hamer.* Amsterdam: 1943.

Henderson, G. *Survival of Belief Among the Celts.* Glasgow: 1911.

Hervey, T. K. *The Book of Christmas.* London: William Spooner, 1836.

Hole, C. *Christmas and Its Customs.* M. Barrows & Co., 1958.

Holwerda, Dr. J. H. *Geschiedenis Van Nederlands.* 8 vol. Amsterdam: Uitgevery Joost Van De Vondel N.V., 1935.

Honig, Dr. G. N. *De Vroege Middeleeuwen In Holland.* Amsterdam: Heemschut Serie, Alert De Lange, 1947.

Hornung, C. P., ed. *An Oldfashioned Christmas in Illustration and Decoration.* NY: Dover Publications, Inc.,1970.

Horst, C. F. V/D. *Het Boek Der Helden.* Utrecht, The Netherlands: W. De Haan, 1930.

Hottes, C. A. *1001 Christmas Facts and Fancies.* T. De La Mare Co., 1954.

Hough, P. M. *Dutch Life in Town and Country.* London: 1906.

Innes, H. *Scandanavia.* Life World Library. Time Inc., 1963.

Innes, H. *Handbook of the Nations.* Life World Library. Time Inc., 1966.

Jansen, J. N. *De Duivel en de Doden.* Baarn, The Netherlands: Anbo Publishers, 1993.

Johnston, M. *Roman Life.* Chicago, IL: Scott, Foresman & Co., 1957.

Josephy, A. M. Jr., ed. *American Heritage Indians.* American Heritage Publishing Co., Inc. and Simon & Schuster, Inc., 1961.

Koenigswald, Dr. G. H. R. "Komt Sinterklaas Uit Turkije?" in *Elzeviers Weekblad.* (1 December 1958).

Kroeber, A. L. *An Anthropologist Looks at History.* Berkeley and Los Angeles, CA: University of California Press, 1966.

Kronfeld, E. M. *Der Weihnachtsbaum.* Oldenburg, 1906.

Krythe, M. R. *All About Christmas.* Harper & Bros., 1954.

Laan, K. T. *Folkloristisch Woordenboek.* The Hague, The Netherlands: 1974.

Landtmann, G. *The Origin of the Inequality in the Social Classes.* NY: Greenwood Press, 1968.

Larousse Encyclopedia of Mythology. UK: The Hamlyn Publishing Group Ltd., 1974.

Lawick-Goodall, J. V. *My Friends the Wild Chimpanzees.* Washington, DC: National Geographic Society, 1967.

Lawick-Goodall, J. V. *In the Shadow of Man.* NY: Dell, 1971.

Lewy, G. *Religion and Revolution.* NY: Oxford University Press, 1974.

Lowen, A. *The Language of the Body.* NY: Collier Books, 1958.

Manhardt, W. *Der Baumkultus der Germanen und Ihre Nachbarstaemme.* Berlin, 1875.

Masters, R. E. L. *Eros and Evil: The Sexual Psychopathology of Witchcraft.* NY: Julien Press, 1962.

Maters, H. *Herinneringen aan Sinterklaas.* Netherlands America Society Newsletter, Dec. 1989.

Meszger, W. *Sankt Nicolaus, Schwabenberg Verlag.* Germany: 1993.

Miles, C. A. *Christmas Customs and Traditions.* NY: Dover Publications, Inc., 1976. (A re-publication of *Christmas in Ritual and Tradition, Christian and Pagan,* originally published by T. Fisher Unwin in 1912.)

Miller, D. L. *Gods and Games.* NY: The World Publishing Company, 1970.

Miller, R. *In Search of Santa Claus.* No publisher, no date.

Monseur, E. *Le Folklore Wallon.* 1892.

Morris, H. S. *In the Yule Log Glow.* 4 vol. J. B. Lippincott, 1892.

Morris, R. *The New World.* Vol. 1, The New Life History of the USA. Time, Inc. Book Division, 1963.

Morris, R. *The Making of a Nation.* Vol. 2, The New Life History of the USA. Time, Inc. Book Division, 1963.

Morris, W., and M. *Dictionary of Word and Phrase Origins.* NY: Harper & Row Publishers, 1962.

Motley, Dr. J. L. *The Rise of the Dutch Republic.* 4 vol. NY: Harper Bros., 1883.

Motley, Dr. J. L. *History of the United Netherlands.* 3 vol. NY: Harper Bros., 1883.

Murdock, G. P. *Our Primitive Contemporaries.* NY: Macmillan, 1934.

Murray, M. A. *The God of the Witches.* NY: Oxford University Press, 1970.

Murray, M. A. *Witch Culture in Western Europe.* 1921.

Newark, T. *The Barbarians.* UK: Blanford Press, 1985.

Nierop, H. V. *Santa Claus the Dutch Way.* NY: The Netherlands Information Service, 1962.

Olson, R. *Clan and Moiety in Native America.* Berkeley, CA: University of California Publications in American Archeology and Ethnology, 1933.

Phillips, J. B. *The New Testament in Modern English.* NY: The Macmillan Co., 1959.

Piggott, S. *Ancient Europe.* Chicago, IL: Aldine Publishing Co., 1965.

Platt, C. *The Atlas of Medieval Man.* London: 1979.

Radin, P. *Primitive Man as a Philosopher.* NY: Dover, 1957.

Rausing, G. *The Bow.* Lund, Sweden: 1967.

Reiche, R. *Sexuality and Class Struggle.* London: 1970.

Renterghem, T. V. *The Four Gospels Analysis.* Los Angeles, CA: G. Stevens Productions, 1961. (Research report. Ten copies made.)

Renterghem, T. V. *And Jesus Speaks.* Los Angeles, CA: G. Stevens Productions, 1961. (Ten copies made.)

Renterghem, T. V. "A Detective Story: The True Origins of Sinter-Klaas & Zwarte Piet." *N. A. S. News,* 1986.

The Revised Standard Version of The Holy Bible. NY: Thomas Nelson and Sons, 1953.

Reydon, H. *Het Zonnerad.* Utrecht, The Netherlands: N. E. N. A. S. U., 1936.

Robinson, J. *Body Packaging.* CA: Elysium Growth Press, 1988.

Romein, Dr. J. *De Lage Landen Bij de Zee.* Utrecht, The Netherlands: W. De Haan, 1934.

Ross, L. "The Myth That Things are Getting Better." *New York Review of Books* (12 August 1972).

Rooijakkers, G., I. Dresen-Coenen, and M. Geerdes. *Duivelsbeelden Een Cultuurhistorische Speurtocht Door De Lage Landen.* The Netherlands: Ambo Publishers Baarn, 1994.

Sandys, W. *Christmastide, Its History, Festivities, and Carols.* John Russell Smith, no date.

Schilstra, J. J. *Prenten in Hout.* The Netherlands: Uitgevery De Tijdstroom B. V., 1985.

Schmookler, A. B. *The Parable of the Tribes.* Boston, MA: Houghton Mifflin Co., 1984.

Schultz, W. *Altgermanische Kultur in Wort und Bild.* Munich: J. F. Lehman Verl., 1935.

Service, E. R. *A Profile of Primitive Culture.* NY: Harper, 1958.

Severin, T. *Vanishing Primitive Man.* NY: 1970.

Seward, D. *The Monks of War.* Suffolk, UK: Paladin, 1972.

Shakespeare, W. *The Complete Works of William Shakespeare.* B. Blackwell, ed. Oxford: Shakespeare Head Press, 1934.

Sittwell, N. H. H. *The World the Romans Knew.* London: Hamish Hamilton, 1984.

Spears, R. A. *Slang and Euphemism Dictionary.* NY: Jonathan David Publishers, Inc., 1981.

Spicer, D. *Festivals of Western Europe.* H. W. Wilson Co., 1958.

Steven, W. A., and E. De Witt-Burton. *A Harmony of the Gospels.* NY: Charles Scribner's Sons, 1932.

Stolz, A. *Shamanen, Ekstase Und Jenseits-Symbolik, Du-Mont Buchverlag.* Cologne, Germany: 1988.

Tacitus. *Annales.* (Many translations available.)

Taylor, L. R. *The Divinity of the Roman Emperors.* Monographs no. 1. The American Philosophical Association, Middletown: 1931.

Thompson, E. A. *The Early Germans.* Oxford: 1965.

Thompson, E. A. *The Visigoths in the Time of Ulfila.* Oxford: 1965.

Tille, A. *Yule and Christmas.* London: 1899.

Time-Life Books. *The Celts.* The Emergence of Man Series. 1974.

Time-Life Books. *Cro-Magnon Man.* The Emergence of Man Series. 1973.

Time-Life Books. *The First Men.* The Emergence of Man Series. 1973.

Time-Life Books. *The Neanderthals*. The Emergence of Man Series. 1973.

Time-Life Books. *The Northmen*. The Emergence of Man Series. 1974.

Time-Life Books. *The Sea Traders*. The Emergence of Man Series. 1974.

Time-Life, Inc. *The Life Book of Christmas*. 3 volumes. NY: Time, Inc., 1963.

Tirion, I. *Hedendaagsche Historie of Tegenwoordige Staat van alle Volkeren*. Part 18. Amsterdam: 1750.

Todd, M. *The Northern Barbarians BC 100 to AD 300*. London: 1975.

Tryckare, T. *The Vikings*. Gothenburg, Sweden: Cagner & Co., 1966.

Turnbull, C. M. *The Forest People*. NY: Simon & Schuster, 1962.

Vaux O. P. *Ancient Israel, Its Life and Institutions*. NY: McGraw-Hill Book Co., Inc., no date.

Veen, Dr. P. A. F. *Entymologisch Woordenbook*. Utrecht/Antwerpen: Van Dale Lexicografie B. V., 1991.

Vlaming, M., and F. Witte. *Van Demonen en Ander Gedonderjaag*. Texel, Holland: 1980.

Vloberg, M. *Les Noels de France*. Paris: B. Arthaud, 1953.

Vries, J. De. *De Wetenschap der Volkskunde*. Amsterdam: 1941.

Waechter, J. *Man Before History*. London: 1976.

Wallace-Hadrill, J. M. *The Barbarian West 400-1000*. London: 1967.

Warner, R. *Men and Gods*. Harmondsworth: Penguin Books, 1952.

Watts, A. W. *The Way of Zen.* NY: Pantheon Books, Inc., 1957.

Webster, A. M. *Webster's New International Dictionary of the English Language.* 2nd ed., unabridged. C. Miriam Company Publishers, 1937.

Wells, H. G. *The Outline of History.* NY: Garden City Books, 1949.

Wendt, H. *In Search of Adam: The Story of Man's Search for Truth About his Earliest Ancestors.* Boston, MA: Houghton Mifflin, 1956.

Wernecke, H. H. *Christmas Customs Around the World.* Westminster Press, 1959.

Wheelis, A. *The End of the Modern Age.* NY: Basic Books, 1971.

Wilson, D. *The Family Christmas Book.* Prentice Hall, 1957.

Wood, D. R. *Genesis.* Kent, UK: The Balan Press, 1985.

Wood, M. *In Search of the Dark Ages.* Facts on File Publications, 1987.

Index

Gaia, xvi, xviii, 22, 85, 148, 152, 154

Garden of Eden, 10, 26

Germany, Germans, 10, 13, 24-27, 32, 37, 45-48, 66, 69, 71, 74-77, 83, 88-89, 93, 96-99, 103, 105, 108, 110-112, 116-119, 122, 124-126, 154, 168, 171, 184

God(s), xviii, xxi, 7, 10, 13, 16-17, 21-24, 26-28, 36-37, 42, 47, 53, 57, 60-61, 66, 69-72, 76, 78, 81-82, 85-86, 88-89, 93, 96-97, 102-103, 105, 108, 111-112, 116, 118-119, 121-122, 124, 150-152, 154-155, 157, 159, 163-164, 168-169, 172, 184, 186

Godot, 155

Golden Bough, 42, 165

Grampus, 98, 105

Great forest, 22, 126

Greek(s), 10-11, 37, 42, 57, 63, 73, 88, 103, 108, 141, 166

Gypsies, 73, 84

Hammer, Thor's, 66

Hans Trapp, 98, 105

Helia, 42

Hell, 5, 47, 91, 97, 100

Hemp, 57, 144-145

Henry VIII, King, 66-67, 163

Herne and Herne/Pan, xvii, 25-27, 54, 58-59, 61, 63, 65-66, 69, 72, 77-80, 85-93, 96-97, 100, 102-104, 112-116, 122, 125-127, 153-154

Heroes, 18, 23, 26, 61, 86

Hitler, Adolf, 149

Holland, 7, 33, 90, 97-99, 111, 117, 124, 165-166, 172

Holocaust, 16, 81

Horned One, 65, 91, 112, 143

Horse(s)
Holy White, 97
Schimmel, 111-112
wild, 22, 39, 65, 75, 91, 109, 111-112, 118, 120, 124, 126, 129, 136, 139, 144, 168, 186

Ice Age, 35-36, 121, 129

Inbreeding, 21

Indians (North American), 10, 18, 22, 61, 65, 163, 167

Indo-European(s), 13, 26-27, 43, 72

Inquisition, 16, 27, 90-91, 109, 125, 153-154

Inuit, 18, 76, 146

Invaders, 16, 74-75, 77

Irving, Washington, 52

Isis and Horus, 27, 71-72

Jesus, xxi, 13, 25, 28, 46, 61, 72, 77, 81, 89, 122, 151, 164, 170

Jews, 25, 84

Judeo-Christian, 24, 28

Kalendea, 42

Kalends, 141

Klas Buer, 105

Klaubau, 103

Klaus, 96, 98

Klawes, 98, 105

Knecht Ruprecht, 54, 103, 116

Knickerbocker History, 52

Knowledge, 4, 6, 8, 10, 17, 23, 26, 28, 57, 60-61, 73, 81, 148-150, 153-154, 157

Lapps, 76, 84, 146

Laws of Nature, 149-150

Lebkuchen, 124

Legend(s), 10, 48, 52, 77, 79, 82, 84, 88, 96, 101, 112, 160, 166, 184, 186

Orgies, 21, 76, 86, 147

Overpopulation, 23, 153

Pagan, xxi, xv, 7, 13-14, 17-18, 21, 23, 25, 27-28, 30, 33, 36-39, 41-42, 44-48, 66, 69, 71, 74, 77, 80, 84, 90-91, 93, 96-97, 100, 102-103, 105, 110-112, 115-119, 121-123, 125, 142, 153, 159-160, 163, 168, 186

Pan, xvii, 24-27, 54, 58, 61, 63, 65-66, 69, 78-80, 83-86, 88-93, 96-97, 100, 103, 112, 114-116, 125, 127, 153-154

Paradise, 8, 10, 42

Pelz Nickel, 103

Pelzmaerte, 105

Persia, 24

Persians, 43

Pilgrim(s), 33, 41

Pinora, 96

Poison(s), 23, 73, 82

Pollution, 152-153

Pomander, 47

Pope Gregorius the Great, 32, 36, 117

Poseidon, 96

Priapus, 88

Priest(s), 9, 26, 28, 30, 32, 47, 60-61, 72, 77, 85-86, 103, 147, 150-151, 159

Prometheus, 10-11, 28

Protestant(s), 7, 27, 47, 90-91, 93, 108, 125

Puck, 80, 89, 116

Puritans, 41, 73, 76, 90, 125, 154

Pygmies, 73, 82, 84

Racial prejudice, 102

Rape, 37, 125, 147

Reed flute, 84

Reformation, 27, 46, 90-91, 125

Religion, xvii, 15-16, 18-19, 21-23, 26-28, 33, 53, 66-68, 71-72, 74, 76-78, 81, 88-90, 93, 96-97, 103, 108-110, 117, 120, 122-124, 150, 153, 159, 162, 165, 168

Ritual

fertility, 7, 9-10, 24, 37, 39, 42-43, 47, 59, 63, 66-68, 74, 87-89, 109, 112, 122, 138, 143, 159

misuse of, 36, 148

teaching, 72, 149, 153

Robin Goodfellow, 80, 116

Robin Hood, 77, 84, 103, 127

Roman numerals, 130

Roman, 9, 11, 17, 25, 27-28, 32, 37, 41, 46, 69-72, 74, 83, 86, 89-91, 96, 108, 110, 112, 118, 130, 141, 153, 165-167, 171, 184

Rooster, 7, 25, 87, 122-123

Roots, xvi, xxi, 9, 22, 48, 53, 67, 107, 109, 111, 131, 134, 139, 146-147

Ruling classes, 61, 65, 108

Rune(s), 124

Rushdie, Salman, 82, 150

Russia, 30, 33, 58, 86, 126

Sabine maidens, 37, 74

Sacrifice

human, 5, 21-23, 26, 76, 93, 121, 151, 153, 155, 162, 165

animal, 8, 10, 19, 22-23, 26, 43, 52, 58, 65, 76, 85-86, 89, 93, 109, 117-118, 121-123, 125-126, 131, 135, 144, 148, 154, 162

Index

182

Illustration
Credits

An effort has been made to trace the ownership and/or copyright holder of all illustrations included in this book. We apologize for any errors or omissions. Upon notification, we will make appropriate acknowledgements in subsequent editions.

Illustrations are listed by page number, from top to bottom and left to right.

Page xvii—Photos: T. van Renterghem. 6—T. van Renterghem. 7—Photo: Michael Guttman. Photo: T. van Renterghem. Photo: T. van Renterghem. 11—from Thomas Bulfinch, *The Age of Fable*, 1903. From John Clark Ridpath, *Ridpath's History of the World*, 1897. 12—

Alfred Hunt, from *The Illustrated London News*, 1876. From *The Saturday Evening Post*, 1867. 17—Tapestry fragment drawn by Alexandra Lumen. From John Clark Ridpath, *Ridpath's History of the World*, 1897. Photo: T. van Renterghem. 20—Tom Grewe. 25—Anne Marie Garrison. 31—Tom Grewe after a sketch by T. van Renterghem. Tom Grewe after a sketch by T. van Renterghem. From *Harter's Pictoral Archive*, 1978. 38—H. Leutemann, from John Clark Ridpath, *Ridpath's History of the World*, 1897. From *Ballou's Pictorial Drawingroom Companion*, 1853. From *Plants and Flowers*, Alan E Bessette and William K Chapman, editors, 1992. 39—From *An Old-Fashioned Christmas in Illustration & Decoration*, Clarence P. Hornung, editor, 1975. From Charles Dickens, *Pickwick Papers*, 1838. 40—From *An Old-Fashioned Christmas in Illustration & Decoration*, Clarence P. Hornung, editor, 1975. 44—Photo: Courtesy Heemkunde-Denekamp Foundation. Tom Grewe. Photo: T. van Renterghem. 45—Courtesy Germanisches National Museum Nurnberg. Nineteenth-century French engraving. 54—Boyd, from Clement C. Moore, *A Visit from St. Nicholas*, 1848. Thomas Nast, from *Harper's Weekly*, 1866. 55—Thomas Nast, from *Harper's Weekly*, 1880. Thomas Nast, from *Harper's Weekly*, 1871. 56—Haddon Sundblom for the Coca-Cola Company; used by permission (Coca-Cola is a registered trademark of the Coca-Cola Company). 58—Courtesy Den Haag, Koninklijke Bibliotheek 54 B 17-18 (modifications by T. van Renterghem). 59—Photos: From Margaret A. Murray, *God of the Witches*. 62—J. A. Pasquier, from *Illustrated London News*, 1858. From Margaret A. Murray, *God of the Witches*. 63—From Margaret A. Murray, *God of the Witches*. Tom Grewe. From Margaret A. Murray, *God of the Witches*. 64—From Margaret A. Murray, *God of the Witches*. From Margaret A. Murray, *God of the Witches*. After Ariege. 67—From Braun and Schneider, *Costumes of All Nations*, 1907. From Jost Amman, *Kunstbüchlin*, 1599. 68—Tom Grewe after a sketch by T. van Renterghem. Tom Grewe after a sketch by T. van Renterghem. Thomas Nast, from *Harper's Weekly*, 1870. 74—From John Clark Ridpath, *Ridpath's History of the World*, 1897. Eliaphas Levi, *Dogme et Rituel de la Houte Magie*, 1856. From Fred Gettings, *Secret Symbolism in Occult Art*, 1987. Used by permission. 75—T. van Renterghem. Tom Grewe after Jean Bourdichon. 78—Tom Grewe. From Richard Huber, *Treasury of Fantastic and Mythological Creatures*, 1981. Tom Grewe. 79—From Anna-Marie Ferguson, *Legend: The Arthurian Tarot*, 1995. Used by permission. Eighteenth-century tarot card. Tom Grewe after a fifteenth-century tarot card. 80—From *An Old-Fashioned Christmas in Illustration & Decoration*, Clarence P. Hornung, editor, 1975. Medieval woodcut. 83—Tom Grewe after a Roman freize. 87—Photo: T. van Renterghem. Photo: T. van Renterghem. Tom Grewe after a nineteenth-century painting. 92—Photos: Courtesy Charles Breyer, Arbeiders Pers, release courtesy *Rotterdams Dagblad*. 98—Franz Regis Goz, 1784. 99—Photos: Courtesy T. van Renterghem. 101—Courtesy Marilyn Matheny. 104—From Charles Dickens, *A Christmas Carol*, 1845. 113—Nineteeth-century postcard, property of T. van Renterghem. 114—From *Illustrated London News*. 115—James Godwin, from *Illustrated London News*, 1864. 119—Eighteenth-century print courtesy T. van Renterghem. Randolph Caldecott, *Old Christmas*, 1875. 120—Photo: Courtesy Charles Breyer, Arbeiders Pers, release courtesy *Rotterdams Dagblad*. From Margaret A. Murray, *God of the Witches*. 123—Arthur Rackham, 1912. Arthur Rackham, 1907. Photo: T. van Renterghem. 156—Photo: David Holt.

On the following page you will find listed, with their current prices, some of the books now available on related subjects. Your book dealer stocks most of these and will stock new titles in the Llewellyn series as they become available. We urge your patronage.

TO GET A FREE CATALOG

You are invited to write for our bi-monthly news magazine/catalog, *Llewellyn's New Worlds of Mind and Spirit*. A sample copy is free, and it will continue coming to you at no cost as long as you are an active mail customer. Or you may subscribe for just $10 in the United States and Canada ($20 overseas, first class mail). Many bookstores also have *New Worlds* available to their customers. Ask for it.

In *New Worlds* you will find news and features about new books, tapes and services; announcements of meetings and seminars; helpful articles; author interviews and much more. Write to:

Llewellyn's New Worlds of Mind and Spirit
P.O. Box 64383-K765, St. Paul, MN 55164-0383, U.S.A.

TO ORDER BOOKS AND TAPES

If your book store does not carry the titles described on the following pages, you may order them directly from Llewellyn by sending the full price in U.S. funds, plus postage and handling (see below).

Credit Card Orders: VISA, MasterCard, American Express are accepted. Call us toll-free within the United States and Canada at 1-800-THE-MOON.

Special Group Discount: Because there is a great deal of interest in group discussion and study of the subject matter of this book, we offer a 20% quantity discount to group leaders or agents. Our Special Quantity Price for a minimum order of five copies of *When Santa Was a Shaman* is $67.80 cash-with-order. Include postage and handling charges noted below.

Postage and Handling: Include $4 postage and handling for orders $15 and under; $5 for orders *over* $15. There are no postage and handling charges for orders over $100. Postage and handling rates are subject to change. We ship UPS whenever possible within the continental United States; delivery is guaranteed. Please provide your street address as UPS does not deliver to P.O. boxes. Orders shipped to Alaska, Hawaii, Canada, Mexico and Puerto Rico will be sent via first class mail. Allow 4-6 weeks for delivery.

International Orders: Airmail – add retail price of each book and $5 for each non-book item (audiotapes, etc.); Surface mail – add $1 per item.

Minnesota residents add 7% sales tax.

Mail orders to:
Llewellyn Worldwide
P.O. Box 64383-K765
St. Paul, MN 55164-0383, U.S.A.

For customer service, call (612) 291-1970.

HIS STORY
Masculinity in the Post-Patriarchal World
Nicholas R. Mann

His Story was written for men of European descent who are seeking a new definition of being. The patriarchal worldview dominating Western thought has cut men off from the traditions which once directly connected them to the nature of their masculinity. This book offers them a means to locate and connect with their birthright—the "native tradition" that lives in the deepest core of their being—by drawing on the pre-Christian era's conception of a man's true masculine nature. *His Story* contrasts patriarchal and pre-patriarchal ideas about masculine identity, self-definition, sexuality, symbology and spirituality—then provides a wealth of information on traditions and mythology that encompass many masculine archetypes, from those of the Grail legends to the Green Man, the Wild Man and the Horned God. Finally, the book reveals how men can connect again with these traditions and their own inherent source of personal power, thus transforming their relationships to those around them and to the world.

1-56718-458-8, 336 pgs., 6 x 9, softbound $16.95

LEGEND
The Arthurian Tarot
Anna-Marie Ferguson

Gallery artist and writer Anna-Marie Ferguson has paired the ancient divinatory system of the tarot with the Arthurian myth to create *Legend: The Arthurian Tarot.* The exquisitely beautiful watercolor paintings of this tarot deck illustrate characters, places and tales from the legends that blend traditional tarot symbolism with the Pagan and Christian symbolism that are equally significant elements of this myth. Each card represents the Arthurian counterpart to tarot's traditional figures, such as Merlin as the Magician, Morgan le Fay as the Moon, Mordred as the King of Swords and Arthur as the Emperor. Accompanying the deck is a decorative layout sheet in the format of the Celtic Cross to inspire and guide your readings, as well as the book *Keeper of Words,* which lists the divinatory meanings of the cards, the cards' symbolism and the telling of the legend associated with each card.

1-56718-267-4, Book: 272 pgs., 6 x 9, illus., softbound,
Deck: 78 full-color cards,
Layout Sheet: 18" x 24", four-color $34.95